CONVERSATIONS

WITH

DOG

Adventures of a 4 Legged Guru

An Inspirational
Novel

By
Jonathan Robinson

GO TO www.FindingHappiness.com TO GET THE ABSOLUTE BEST WAYS TO EASILY BOOST HAPPINESS IN UNDER TWO MINUTES.

Author: Jonathan Robinson
Title: Conversations With Dog: Adventures of a 4 Legged Guru

Printed in the United States of America.

Design: Marina May
Book Interior and E-book Design
by Amit Dey | amitdey2528@gmail.com

First Printing: September 2019

Acknowledgements and Dedication

To all the dogs I've ever owned, especially Rama and Sophie, and to all those who love a dog or help them to thrive.

Table of Contents

CHAPTER 1

Chasing Your Tail

"Dogs do speak,
but only to those who know
how to listen."

Waking up in a hospital and not having a clue as to why or how you got there is not a good way to start a day. All I knew was that my head throbbed, my body ached, and a middle-aged nurse looked concerned as she monitored my vitals on the instrument panel next to my bed.

"What am I doing here?" I heard myself murmur to her.

The nurse gave me a look of both concern and pity. "You're lucky to be alive," she said. "You should never mix alcohol with sleeping pills. Were you trying to kill yourself, Mr. Mosely?"

Good question. I wasn't consciously trying to do myself in, but looking back, I guess you could say I was having a severe midlife crisis. Of course, those words don't come close to describing a life in free fall. Waking up to the question, "Were you trying to kill yourself?" is a good indication that something needs to change. Little did I realize at the time that those words would be the beginning of a whole new life for me. Yet, I later found out that being documented as a suicide risk had implications I never could have imagined. In fact, it impacted what would happen to the greatest love of my life—my dog, Happy. But more about that later.

Suffice to say, at 49-years-old, I found myself alone and almost unable to get out of bed. Each morning, I battled my six-foot-tall body to somehow inch slowly towards a warm shower—just so I wouldn't get stuck in bed for the entire day. When I looked in the mirror, I could barely recognize the brown and gray-haired man with the sunken eyes. Then, one night soon after Marcia, my ex-wife, kicked me out of the house, I began drinking heavily. When a few months of drinking failed to numb my pain, I evidently downed a few sleeping pills. If it weren't for my housekeeper calling 911 when she saw my body in the morning, I may have never woken up again.

Marcia and I had been separated about a year. The divorce papers hadn't been signed yet because we were still arguing over who got what from our 22-year marriage. There's probably no such thing as an easy divorce, but ours had turned into a prolonged dogfight. I felt like a man slowly bleeding to death. I was bitter, depressed, and I no longer felt the will to live. It was scary.

Before they discharged me from the hospital, they even made me sign a "contract" that I wouldn't kill myself. I had no idea such a contract could later be used *against* me in a court of law. Some lessons you just gotta learn the hard way...

Fortunately, once I got a taxi back to my home, a hopeful thought sprang to mind. How this thought came to my mind, I can't really say. I guess some things are simply given by grace. I clearly remember hearing the voice in my head say, "Why don't you get a dog?" I smiled at the thought. I knew if I had a dog to take care of, I'd be a lot less likely to do something stupid like try to hurt myself. Thus began my life-changing journey, punctuaed by all kinds of strange twists and turns.

I hadn't lived with a dog since I was a kid, so I didn't really know what to look for in a canine companion. I figured that going for a drive might send my blues away, so once the taxi delivered me to my house, I drove my Prius the six miles to the local animal shelter. As I parked my car, I heard the clamoring of a hundred barking dogs. I hesitatingly stepped into the shelter's office and told the attendant I *needed* a dog. The elderly man eyed me suspiciously, then grabbed a ring full of keys and led me down a long corridor. Seeing row upon row of dogs lined up in cages made me want to run away and drive back home. But since I had driven all that way, I figured I'd take a quick look around.

As I strolled past a bunch of cages, my heavy heart sank even further into despair. It was hard to see so many dogs locked up with hardly any room to move around. Then, as I looked down the corridor, I noticed a smallish, golden dog a few cages up who was tracking my every movement. She was quiet, but not shy. As soon as our eyes locked onto each other, her entire body wagged in delight. She seemed so filled with joy that I thought she might explode out of her crate. Somehow, I immediately knew in my heart that she was "the one." I don't know how she managed to squeeze so much love into those little dark brown eyes. When I saw her light up at my gaze, my heart sprang open like it had been released from a small cage.

I asked the gray-haired man leading me around, "What kind of dog is that one?" while pointing to this beautiful golden dog.

The man gave me a puzzled look. "Don't really know. She sure is cute, though; looks a bit like a Golden Retriever, just smaller. Maybe she has some Cocker in her."

I felt obligated to ask the man some questions about this dog before I made my decision. "Do you know how old she is?"

"Not really," he began. "She kind of looks like a puppy, but our vet looked her over when she came in and said she was likely three or four-years-old. The vet also said she might have been abused by her former owner, but I don't know the story. She has a slight limp due to a hurt back leg, but other than that, she seems in good health. She's very smart. You can tell by the way she is always trying to figure out what's going on. Unfortunately, she's been here about a month, so she don't have much longer..."

My heart skipped a beat, like I had just been told my life had been threatened. "What do you *mean* she doesn't have much longer?"

The elderly man averted my gaze. He looked out over the row of cages. A melancholy descended over his face. "Sad to say we just have too many dogs. If a dog isn't taken after about a month, we have to put 'em down." The elderly gentleman took a slow, deep breath. Then he looked at me squarely. "Sure is a shame. She's so cute with those big brown eyes and floppy ears. She's quite affectionate too. I'm surprised no one's taken her yet. I'd hate to see her put down..."

That sealed the deal. I felt like he was threatening my *child*. There was no way I was going to allow them to kill this innocent little girl. "I'll take her," I heard myself say, and with those words I felt a great sense of relief.

The elderly man unlocked her little crate. I got down on one knee to properly greet this 25-pound being of unbridled enthusiasm. I was immediately rewarded with a face full of licks. It was like the reunion of two longtime lovers. When this little girl wasn't licking my face, she was barking in celebration. Admittedly, a couple of times I even playfully barked back at her. After a few minutes of mutual merriment, the three of us joyfully walked to the office and took care of the paperwork.

They had no official history on her, so she had to get fully registered. All they knew about her was her approximate age and that a police officer had brought her in as an abandoned dog with no collar. Besides having a new friend and companion, I felt proud to have rescued this fur ball of delight. Within twenty minutes, this little Golden girl was happily enjoying the ride home to my house. By the time she was home in my lap, I had developed a severe case of puppy love.

At first, I didn't know what to name this Golden girl. Fortunately, when I initially walked her around the neighborhood, three people commented on how happy she seemed so, in a way, she named herself.

The first month I had Happy, she definitely made me a bit less depressed. After all, her enthusiasm and sheer joy were contagious. Happy started to teach me about happiness from the moment she entered my life. No amount of Prozac had managed to have half the effect she had on me. She'd wake me up each morning at seven a.m. with a face full of licks. Ironically, I don't care for having my face licked, which is why her insistent licks worked so well to get me out of bed! I liked to tell my friends who would fall victim to her unrelenting affection that "the poor girl can't hold her licker."

Anyway, after a month of being around this delightful little being, a strange thought came to me. I thought, "Wouldn't it be great if I could be even half as happy as she is?" Rather than quickly dismiss the notion, I felt deeply impacted by it. Was it possible that a human—me—could learn to be almost as joyous as his dog? While I was obviously a million miles away from that goal, it seemed *theoretically* possible. So, while eyeing Happy's look of ecstasy while I rubbed her belly, I decided to do something I had rarely done in my adult life: I began to pray.

I don't remember the exact prayer. The feeling behind it was more important than the specific words. Yet, if I had to put into words the sentiment I expressed that day, it would go something like this:

"Dear God,

Thank you so much for bringing Happy into my life. Although I am still suffering from depression, I see the possibility of someday feeling good again. Please allow me to humble myself and learn from this little girl how to truly be happy. May I be open to hearing the messages she has to teach me about enjoying each moment in my life. May I listen to her for how to be more loving, peaceful, and joyous...I pray that with your and her help, I can learn to be happy again. Amen."

That was it. Since I was not used to praying, I didn't really know what to expect. I continued rubbing Happy's belly, and as I did, I had the thought that rubbing her belly might be like rubbing the lamp of a genie—who knew what wishes or magical forces might be unleashed.

I don't know whether it was God or a magic genie or simply my own subconscious mind, but I immediately began to notice how blissful Happy was most of the time. Being a human being, I had thought of myself as much higher up the evolutionary ladder than a dog—no matter how enlightened that dog happened to be. Yet, I remember reading a quote from the Dalai Lama that said something like, "The goal of life is to be happy, and to live your life in a way that makes others happy." Well, by that standard, my little pooch was light years ahead of me.

I'm lucky in that, being an accountant in private practice, I get to work out of an office in my house. This allowed me to spend a lot of time watching Happy's daily habits. I soon began to notice that she and I were about as different as two beings could be. If men are from Mars and women are from Venus, then Golden Retrievers are from a whole other galaxy. It didn't take long for me to realize that, compared to Happy, I was an unhappy mess. Happy's daily life consisted of mostly rest, play, and loving connection. On the other hand, my life consisted of a lot of worry, rushing around, and feeling frustrated. I quickly surmised that having large pre-frontal lobes is not particularly a helpful tool on the road to happiness.

As I write this story of my adventures with Happy, it has been about a year since I found her that fateful day. Having just woken up in a hospital, I found her—or she found me-- at the darkest time in my life. Since then she quickly became my guru, my best friend, my playmate, and even my confidant. I know all of this can sound pretty weird, like maybe I'm a bit over attached to my dog. But it's more than that. In fact, what I'm about to tell you will likely make you think I'm a total crackpot. I even hesitated writing about what I'm about to tell you, but then I figured my story might help to inspire some other person going through a tough time. Okay, here goes: my dog *talks* to me. I mean I hear her speak to me inside my head. I'm serious.

Of course, when I began hearing her voice in my head, I figured there was a screw loose in my brain. But I noticed that the innocent voice I was hearing inside my head made a lot of sense, so I decided to listen to it before I checked myself back into the hospital.

I know what you're probably thinking: this guy is one sick puppy. At least that's what *I* would think if someone told me their dog talks to them. But I want you to know I'm a 49-year-old man who has never had a psychotic breakdown. I'm an *accountant* for God's sake—I'm not some woo-woo New Age guy who channels an ancient being. But apparently, as far as I can tell, I channel a small Golden Retriever. She speaks to me in her own voice—it sounds totally different than the normal voice inside my head. Happy tells me all about her world, her joys, her observations of me, even her philosophy. In a very real way, she's my guru.

Perhaps if I tell you *how* I started hearing her voice in my head, you'll be more likely to think I'm not a total kook. It all began a day after my prayer to learn to be as happy as my little Golden girl. As I cuddled Happy contentedly in my lap, a strange thought occurred to me. I thought, "I wonder what Happy's observations of *me* would be?" For a moment, I became open to seeing myself from *her* point of view.

Immediately, I imagined that Happy would think I was very out of touch with my body—largely because I *am* very out of touch with my body. I imagined she'd observe I don't take time to smell the roses—nor much of anything else. I realized that she would notice I don't rest between activities like she does, nor even rest when I'm tired. Then seemingly out of nowhere, my mental daydream was interrupted by a strange sounding voice.

The voice sounded like the light, friendly sound of a five-year-old little girl. At first I thought the voice came from behind me, but I knew that was impossible. I was sitting on a couch, and behind me was a wall. Then I realized the voice came from inside me, but it sure didn't sound like any voice I'd ever heard before inside my head. Besides, the actual words I heard were not words I had ever spoken or thought of. In a strangely innocent lilting sound, I perceived the words "I think you are very loving, but you spend a lot of time chasing your tail."

I immediately thought I had taken my mental and emotional problems to a whole new level. Being depressed is one thing, but hearing your dog's voice in your head is reserved for people who are carted away to mental hospitals. I got scared. It didn't help matters when I heard that same innocent voice inside my head say, "Don't be scared. I've always been talking to you; but now you're finally listening."

I looked at Happy contentedly cuddled up in my lap, her big brown eyes looking up at me. She felt like a baby—all relaxed lying on her back, with her belly enjoying my gentle caresses. I looked into her wise brown eyes and said out loud, "Is that really you?"

I didn't really expect an answer, but I got one anyway. Once again, I heard that innocent sounding voice as clearly as if she were lying in my lap—which she was. She said, "Yep, it's me. I'm so happy that you're able to hear me now. Be careful for what you pray for!"

My mind flashed back to the day before when I had prayed to God to be able to listen and learn from Happy. For a moment, I thought I must be dreaming. My reverie was quickly interrupted by the now familiar voice: "You're not dreaming. It's just that the Lord works in mysterious ways. After all, 'dog' is 'God' spelled backwards. I like to think us dogs are especially close to God."

Not only did I have a talking dog, I had a *philosophical* talking dog—with a sense of humor. Having never encountered anything like this before, I didn't really know what to think or do about it. Before I could fully get my bearings, Happy's "voice" announced itself again.

"Do you wanna be all serious and worried, or would you rather play? Come on, let's plaaaaaay! Just go with hearing my voice and don't worry about it. It'll be fun. Try it for a little bit and see what it's like. New things are always scary at first, but I promise you I won't bite."

I continued to sit on the couch, dumbfounded by what was taking place. I thought to myself that at least what Happy was "saying" made some sense. I reasoned that if hearing her voice in my head sent me over the edge, I could always call my psychiatrist. But, for the time being, I was willing to listen to what this "voice" had to say.

"Okay, little girl, let's play ball," I said out loud.

"Yippee!" her voice squealed inside my head. Happy jumped off my lap and gazed at me with a look of joy and delight. "There's so much I want to talk to you about. You've been chasing your tail for so long that it's hard for me to watch you. I just want you to be happy, and play, and enjoy life like I do. It's really not that hard."

Forgetting the strangeness of what was going on, I defensively shot back "Well, it's not that easy."

"Sure it is," Happy quickly replied. "It's the easiest thing in the world. Let me ask you a question. Can you throw a ball?"

Happy often seemed to be asking me this question with her eager eyes and wagging tail. Yet, this time I heard her ask me this question in my head.

"Yes, of course I can throw a ball," I said. I wondered where she was going with this.

Happy's dancing ears and eyes were in full bloom as she looked straight at me. She excitedly began, "If you can throw a ball, you can play. Right now you can moan and growl about problems—and go on chasing your tail, or you can throw a ball and have fun with me. It's not hard."

"But those problems are real," I insisted.

Happy slowly and methodically licked my hand before replying. Later I learned that she'd lick my hand as a way of "softening me up" before she hit me with a verbal sledgehammer.

Once my hand was thoroughly soaked she put her head on my leg, looked up at me and began, "You're hearing my words, but you're not really listening. You said you wanted to be happier. You can't be happy while being grumpy about everything and growling at people who aren't even in the room with you."

Maybe it was the way she had softened my heart, but somehow her message finally got through my thick skull. My "problems" were not *the* problem. It was my continual *thinking* about them--to the exclusion of everything else-- that created my suffering. On the other hand, Happy lived in the moment. She seemed to delight in whatever was right in front of her. She never complained about the past or whimpered about the future.

By now, I was getting a bit used to conversing with my four-legged sage. Even if I was going bananas and making it all up in my head, the conversation seemed to be *going* somewhere. I decided to ask the question I really wanted to know. "Okay, then, the real question I want to know is *how* can I be happier?"

"It's not hard to be happy," she started. "The puppies of your race are happy a lot of the time, so it can't be *that* hard. But as people grow older, that joy can leave. Why do so many humans look so stressed and depressed? I just don't understand. It makes me sad to see people feeling so bad."

I could see that Happy was really saddened by her perception of people's suffering. In an attempt to be helpful, I figured I could finally teach my little pooch some hard fought wisdom. It was obvious to me that she didn't understand all the things people have to contend with. In a compassionate and somewhat condescending tone I began, "Well, Happy, the world is very challenging for people. They lose their joy because, as they get older, they have a lot of problems and responsibilities they need to handle. Also, there are things like war and disease and loss-- and global warming."

Happy raised her head from my lap and looked up at me quizzically. With an innocence that melted my heart, I heard her voice say, "I don't see any war here; I don't see any problems; I don't see any disease. Maybe that's just a story in your head. What I see right here and now is a loving human being cuddling with me. Life is gooooood!" Her tail wagged with enthusiasm.

I had to admit, upon hearing of her world, *my* reality sounded like a nightmare of my own creation. I had almost forgotten that such a simple and obvious world as the one she lived in truly existed.

Then, for the second time that morning, something really strange happened. For a moment, something in me shifted and I "saw" the world from *her* perspective. Sitting there on the couch while gently petting her head, it felt like everything grew very still and quiet. I looked out my window to the trees just outside, noticing that they seemed to glow as they were lit up by the sun. I sensed a world of eternal tranquility. I sensed a world permeated by love. It was so incredibly peaceful! The streaming rays of the setting sun lit up dust particles that floated across the room. It was magical to watch! It was like a huge burden had been lifted from my shoulders. It felt like silence had, in a strange way, become "louder" or more noticeable. I hadn't felt so light and free since I had been a little child.

Happy seemed to pick up on my experience and my thoughts. She finally broke the silence by saying, "My world is a lot like the world of your young ones. So I guess the way to be happier is to become like the puppies of your species."

Happy's words reminded me of what Jesus had once said: "Truly I tell you, anyone who will not receive the kingdom of God like a little child will never enter it."

It was clear to me I had spent many years feeling far away from the experience of a little child. In fact, I had been feeling very, very old. However, I still had hope. From the depths of my hope and faith in something better, I asked another question: "Can you show me how to be like a little child again?"

Happy looked at me with her expectant and playful eyes. "I would loooooove to," was her enthusiastic reply.

My heart sped up in reaction to her excited response. I stopped petting her head, and asked her in a serious tone, "Okay, how do we start?"

In her sprightly voice, she began, "We always start with where we are. There is no other place to start. So, right now, are you feeling better than you felt a while ago?"

I remembered back to just a half hour before. It was not hard to remember what I was up to. As usual, I was throwing a pity party for myself. I was ruminating about how screwed up my life had become, and how it was everyone's fault but my own. Yes, I was now feeling a heck of a lot better than I had been. I was now feeling hopeful, curious, even blessed to have this "conversation" with my own little guru. I reported to Happy that I was feeling much better.

"So, how did you go from stressed and depressed to hopeful and blessed? That's quite a jump for a mopey mutt such as yourself."

I had to admit, it *was* quite a jump. But I didn't really know the answer as to how it had all happened.

Happy saw that I was stumped. She offered, "Here's what you did: you were willing to play ball with me. You noticed the quiet and love underneath all the stories in your head. You let go of growling at things that are not even here. Instead of whimpering, you started to really listen to me."

It was all true. I had somehow managed to take the high road.

Happy continued. "So you played the game and won."

"What game are you talking about Happy?" I wasn't aware I had played a game, but for Happy, almost everything was *some* kind of game.

She began, "I believe you humans call it the hot and cold game. You know the game. You hide a biscuit and then you tell a child when they're getting closer to the biscuit—or 'warmer', or when they're getting 'colder' or farther away. If the child listens to what you say, they soon find the biscuit."

I was confused. I said aloud, "How was I playing the hot and cold game? I don't get it."

Happy patiently explained, "Life is always playing the hot and cold game with us, but this time you really listened to the feedback you were getting. When you were feeling bad earlier, that was Life's way of saying, 'You're freezing! Go in a different direction.' Normally, when bad feelings tell you you're not facing the direction of being happy, you just keep chasing your tail. But this time you didn't. You stopped chasing your tail and moved in a different direction. That led you to a 'warmer' place. Before you knew it, you found what you were looking for—new learning, new love, and new hope."

"I found the biscuit!" I blurted out with real enthusiasm.

"Yes you did, and doesn't it smell—I mean--*feel* good?" Happy wagged her tail approvingly. "So keep listening to how you feel and how people treat you. When you feel love, or peace, or happiness, that's Life's way of saying you're getting warmer. Keep going *that* way. When you feel like growling, or mopey, or whimpering, that's Life's way of saying you've been moving in the wrong direction. It's that simple."

I had to admit I was feeling better than I had felt in a long time. I felt hopeful, even grateful. On one level, nothing in my life had changed, but on another level, *everything* had changed. I asked Happy if she would continue to teach me lessons about how to enjoy life more.

Happy smiled at me with her eyes before I heard her voice in my head: "When the student is ready, the teacher will appear. As long as you're open to learning, you'll be able to learn from me, or for that matter, learn from anyone—even a cat."

With that last statement, Happy jumped off of my lap and ran through the doggie door to our backyard. In the quiet of my living room, I took stock of what had just happened. It had been miraculous! Somehow, I had stepped out of the internal crap I had been living in. I had simply asked for help, and been open to receiving it. I was excited to see where my adventures with a "talking" dog might lead to next....

CHAPTER TWO

Like a Dog with a Bone

Over the next couple of months, I continued to play with the idea that my dog could talk to me. I thought of our conversations as a new form of "play." That seemed to me to be a better explanation than the alternative –which was thinking I might be going bonkers. One day after eating a hearty breakfast, I looked at Happy sitting nearby carefully watching me eat. "You wanna go for a walk?," I asked. Of course, I knew what her answer would be.

"Yes! Yes! Yippee, yesireeee! Let's *go*. Yes. Yes!!" Happy sat obediently in front of me while her wildly wagging tail gave away her true feelings. I attached her retractable leash to her collar as she sat like a firecracker waiting to explode. She liked her leash. For Happy, a leash was a strap that attached to *my* hand so she could lead *me* around. Her whole body wagged in delight as she pleadingly looked up at me. "Where are we going Master Mark?"

Happy calls me "Master Mark" not because I am a master at anything, but because she thinks it's pretty cool how I can make her food magically appear from a lifeless tin can. I often call her "Wiggle Butt" because the force of her wagging tail makes her whole body wiggle. She's not crazy about that name. In fact, when I call her "Wiggle Butt," she'll often reply with her nickname for me—which is "Mopey Mutt." I guess it's well deserved. After all, she has had to work hard to lift my spirits above a daily pity party.

So as "Mopey Mutt" put his hat on, "Wiggle Butt's" tail seemed to push her body forward towards the door like a propeller. When I opened the door, I saw a blur of golden fur sprint out towards the driveway. Fortunately, the 20 foot long leash kept her from being launched into the neighborhood.

My plan was simple. Bring the happiest, most loving being I'd ever known to help me get through a difficult conversation. My ex-wife, Marcia, had called me saying, "We need to talk." Having been married to her for twenty-two years, I knew that was her secret code for "you're in the doghouse." I hated such "talks" the same way Happy loathed going to the vet's office.

Although at this point I'd only had Happy a couple of months, we had already been to the vet three times. Her back right leg had apparently been badly whacked or smashed. She limped on it without complaint, but when I asked her what had happened to her leg, Happy simply said, "I'd rather not talk about it now."

From what I had gathered at the animal shelter, I assumed it had something to do with her former owner. The thought that he or she may have hurt her in this way made my blood boil.

It has been said, "The Lord works in mysterious ways." Well, in this case that's certainly true. A former dog owner, a hurt leg, and a contract saying I would not try to kill myself all conspired to teach me lessons that changed my life. If only I could have understood at the time that such things were part of a cosmic plan, I could have saved myself from a lot of unnecessary suffering. Such is life.

Anyway, Marcia and I agreed to meet at the park near my house. On the way to the park, as Happy sniffed the telephone poles and plants dotting the sidewalk, I began to hear her voice in my head. Even though I had been having these "conversations" with her for a couple of months, when Happy would start "talking" with me, it would still take me by surprise. I never knew what she'd ask me or what she would bring up. She didn't see life the way I did, and I found her way of looking at things to be both fascinating and challenging.

"Master Mark, why do you sit in front of a light screen most of your day?"

"That's part of how I make money to buy things like the food you and I eat." I always enjoyed answering her questions. My answers made me look at my own life as if seeing it for the first time.

"Is that why you sit in front of a light screen at night too?" she asked with amused curiosity.

"No, at night I sometimes look at a light screen to connect with friends on something called Facebook, or I watch TV to be entertained."

Happy stopped walking and gave me her puzzled look--with her head slightly tilted at an angle. She said, "I don't see how you meet friends or are entertained by looking at a light screen."

I thought about it from her perspective and indeed, it did seem weird. I tried to come up with an analogy she could relate to. "Well, when you walk down the street, you smell where your friends have been, and from what I hear, you even know how they're feeling and how their health is from the smells they leave. Well, Facebook is like a human fire hydrant. By staring at the screen, we find out how our friends are doing."

Happy seemed to understand my analogy, although I found it funny to equate Facebook with a fire hydrant where dogs do their "business." I ventured on to explain the allure of television. "TV, for humans, is equivalent to a really good bone. It can keep us busy for hours, and it has an addictive quality to it. It's hard to stop 'chewing' on it until the show we're watching is all done.

Happy appeared satisfied with my answer. I enjoyed coming up with explanatory bridges between her and my world. It made me realize that, even though we were from different species, we had many of the same desires and feelings.

Happy interrupted my thoughts by asking me where we were walking to. For her, there was no need for a destination, but she knew that I always seemed to need a specific place to get to.

"Happy, we're going to the park to meet Marcia, and I brought you along partly because I could really use your help."

"We're going to meet Marcia? Oh boy, oh boy!" she began. "I like Marcia. She smells really good. She gives good belly rubs."

"Oh crap, oh crap, is more like it," I retorted out loud. Sometimes during our conversations I would talk out loud to my little girl, and sometimes I would just direct my thoughts her way. It didn't seem to make any difference to her. Either way, she seemed to pick up on my mood and mental meanderings.

Happy looked up at me questioningly. "What's wrong? It's a beautiful day, there are lots of great smells out, and we're going to see Marcia who is very nice and loving."

I stopped walking for a moment so I could direct my words at my naïve little girl. "What Marcia are you talking about Happy? This is the woman who managed to criticize how I walked, how I ate, how I never cleaned the dishes, and then booted me out of the house that *I* paid for!"

Happy was not about to be persuaded by my anger. She cheerily replied, "That's sooooo in the past. Besides, she treated you that way because you treated *her* that way. I got no bone to pick with Marcia. The couple of times I've seen her, I wag my tail and greet her with a few licks. Since I show her some loving, she smiles and loves me back. You should try it sometime..."

I felt insulted. Getting confronted by Marcia was bad enough. Having my dog insult me on top of it was downright humiliating. "I don't think my giving her a few licks would have quite the same effect on her as when you do it," I cracked dismissively.

Now it was Happy's turn to feel insulted. She looked at me disapprovingly. "There you go again," she began, "making fun of the great wisdom teachings of dogkind. I know you humans have opposing thumbs, and can make food come out of a can, but that doesn't mean you know what's important."

Not only did I seemingly own a "talking" dog, but I owned a dog that knew how to "bite" in disturbing ways. Just my luck. Yet, having endured and then realized the value of Happy's feedback for several weeks, I was willing to hear more of her perspectives.

"Okay," I said. "What do you mean we humans don't know what's important?"

"I mean you don't *know* what's important. You get lost in odd stories in your head and you forget that only love and happiness are what's key. You sometimes laugh at my antics of chasing a ball or excitedly greeting people, but what could be more strange than thinking about your problems while beautiful scenery is passing you by?"

I interrupted her rant. "Well, that's easy for you to say, but you don't have a lot of responsibilities you have to deal with. You don't have to work for a living, or deal with your ex-wife's complaints."

I was pretty sure my explanation would shut her up. I was wrong.

"Exactly!" Happy replied—as if I had suddenly agreed with her. "And *why* don't I have to deal with all those things that you humans have to deal with?"

I didn't really know where she was going with this question, but even though I'm only human, I could still smell a trap. Finally, I figured I'd take the bait. "Okay Happy, why *don't* you have to deal with all that stuff?"

"Because of the power of unconditional love! Love is the greatest, most powerful force in the world. We dogs don't need to work, or pay taxes, or even hunt for our own food anymore because of one reason: love. Love is the target to always aim for. We just love, and by loving, we're taken care of. It's as simple as that."

I hated when she would say, "It's as simple as that." And she said it a lot. From my perspective, it was never *that* simple, but Happy's consistently smiling face and wagging tail made me wonder if her perspectives were more enlightened than my own.

Happy continued, "You know the term 'like a dog with a bone?'"

"Sure."

Happy sat down on her hind legs and looked directly at me with her big, brown eyes. "Well, what does that phrase mean? To me it means that a dog has an ability to focus—to the exclusion of everything else. A dog with a bone is a very happy dog—hint, hint! So when I don't have an actual bone to chew on, I create one! The 'bone' I focus on is simply love. I seek love out no matter how far down it is buried. I protect it. With care and affection, I lick off the dirt that hides the bone. Love is the target to always aim for. As long as there is someone to love, I am like a dog with a bone."

Happy's words that "love is the target to always aim for" reverberated in my mind. It reminded me of a time that I played a one-on-one basketball game with my college roommate Frank. Frank was a varsity basketball player who decided he could humble me by whipping me in a game of basketball. To his surprise, I accepted his challenge—on one condition. I said I'd play him a game of basketball *if* I could bring out a one-ounce gadget and place it anywhere I wanted on the court. Frank agreed to the terms.

When we arrived on the court, I took out my one-ounce gadget—which was a blindfold. I placed the blindfold in a strategic location--over his *eyes*. Then I said, "Let the game begin!" Admittedly, it still ended up being pretty close! Yet, I beat one of the best basketball players in Los Angeles because I knew *exactly* where the target was, and he did not. Happy's words that "love is the target" made me realize I've been running around the court of life with a blindfold on. I had been spending all my energy shooting in the wrong direction. No wonder I wasn't winning at the game of life.

After feeling the impact of this memory, I turned to Happy and said, "All this philosophy sounds good, but I'm a practical person. What do you suggest I do?"

Happy stopped walking again and looked up at me long and hard. I think she was seeing if I was asking her a serious question.

"Well," she began. "You're about to meet up with Marcia. Why not do an experiment?"

Happy would sometimes say words that were new to me or at least used in a different way than I would normally use them. "What kind of experiment?" I wondered.

"The best kind. A Looooooove experiment." Happy grinned as she elongated the word 'love' in my mind. Her twinkling eyes made it clear that she knew something that I did not.

"What are you talking about you crazy pooch?" I liked calling her a crazy pooch, along with about a hundred other nicknames I had made up for her. Whenever I called her by a nickname, it seemed to help me to feel even more connected to her.

"When you meet up with Marcia today, just love her. Be *excited* to see her. Smile. Show her you are overjoyed to see her. Tell her that you've missed her."

I responded reflexively, "But I'm not overjoyed to see her. You want me to *lie*?"

Happy stopped and looked up at me again with those penetrating, heart melting brown eyes. Although she didn't say it in my head, her expression seemed to say, "This poor slob hardly knows anything about love."

She began to patiently explain. ""No I don't want you to lie. I want you to remember that somewhere inside you, you *do* love her. If you weren't so lost in your stories, or your need to growl at her, or your need to be right, you'd remember that you care for her. So lose the stories and take care of her. If you try to take care of her, you'll feel the love—that's the law."

"That's *what* law?" I muttered. Happy sometimes forgot to fully explain things because some things that were super obvious to her were not obvious to me at all.

"The law of love, " she began. We were now walking through an empty field, allowing me to converse with her openly without having to worry if a nosy neighbor thought I was crazy for talking to my dog.

Happy continued, "The law of love states that, if you want to feel more love, take care of someone. You love what you take care of. For example, you love me because you take care of me."

"And you're the cutest nudist Buddhist," I added. Just another one of my many nicknames for my four-legged teacher.

Without missing a beat, Happy responded, "Sure, I don't hurt the eyes, but I'm not as cute as you think I am. After all, I was left in a shelter for a month. People were not falling all over themselves to take me home. Nor do I stop traffic on the street with my cute juice. I'm loveable to you because you take care of me. Because you take care of me, you love me, and because I take care of you, I love you."

Her words hit me hard. It had never made sense to me how the world's cutest dog could have been left in a shelter for so long. Sometimes I'd dismiss what Happy said because I felt that she didn't fully understand my pain. That was before I learned in detail all the horrific things she'd been through with her previous owner. She truly was a master at forgiveness. Now she was trying to pass on her wisdom to me, and the least I could do was take her seriously. Little did I know at the time that I'd later have to learn to forgive someone much harder than Marcia.

Happy interrupted my mental musings. "So when you see Marcia today, love her, adore her, do what you can to take care of her. Be kind. See her as the fragile little human that she is. If you do that, I know it will go really good."

I had to admit that what my canine guru said made some sense. Besides teaching me about the power of forgiveness,

Happy's words and actions had now revealed to me the "law of love."

We were quickly approaching the park. I saw Marcia sitting alone on a far off bench. She looked small and lonely sitting there all by herself. As I focused my eyes on her, I was surprised to notice I felt a sudden twang of compassion for her. I'd been so caught up in my own feelings about the separation that I had never really considered what it was like for Marcia. I imagined it must have been really hard. Alone and starting over at 50. That's gotta be tough. If I knew anything, I knew that one.

When Happy spotted Marcia--and Marcia spotted Happy, they both broke out in a big smile. They'd only met on two occasions, and the last time had been a month ago when Marcia had come by to drop off some bills for me. As Happy got closer to Marcia, she pulled intensely on the leash. Despite being six feet tall and 185 pounds, I was dragged forward by Happy's enthusiasm like I was attached to a sprinting horse.

Before reaching Marcia on the bench, I silently vowed to take on Happy's "experiment." I figured, "What do I have to lose?" I was going to do my best to be kind to Marcia. When Marcia looked up from a book and her eyes caught mine, I started running towards her--pretending to be excited to see her.

Happy reached Marcia before I did. Of course, she did her inevitable lick and love routine. She wagged her tail furiously, and squealed with Joy as Marcia petted her head. Finally, when the loving celebration had run its course, I cheerfully said, "Hi Marcia, it's good to see you." To my surprise, as the words flew out of my mouth, I realized they were actually true. It had been more than four weeks since I'd seen her in person, and it *was* good to see her. I guess I had just covered up those feelings with a bunch of stories in my head.

Marcia seemed a bit surprised by my smile and warm words. She looked up at me suspiciously at first. Then, deciding I was not being sarcastic, she smiled and said, "Well, it's good to see you too Mark. It has been awhile."

Normally, I would have launched into a diatribe about what she was wanting, or a complaint about her lawyer's latest letter to me. Instead, I took Happy's advice—I tried to just appreciate and love her as best I could...

"You're looking great," I began. She did indeed look good. "Thank you for suggesting we get together to talk. It's definitely better to meet in person than to talk through our lawyers."

Marcia looked embarrassed, and her eyes averted from mine. She confessed, "Yeah, sorry about that. You know how lawyers are. I guess I should have reined him in a while ago."

I appreciated her remark. I didn't want to put her on the defensive, so I said, "Well, I understand. Getting divorced is hard and messy. I guess we both had to go through our anger phase. It has been hard on both of us, but hey, here we are. You're an amazing woman. I always had faith that you'd get through the muck and come out shining."

As Marcia's eyes looked into mine, her eyes became moist. She was quiet for a long time. Finally, out of the silence she revealed, "That means a lot to me Mark. Thanks for saying that."

Happy looked up at the two of us approvingly, her tail wagging at a feverish pace.

To my surprise, I felt a real heart warming connection to Marcia. It felt a little vulnerable but also good after so many months of closing down my heart. Then, in a tender tone I said, "I'm hoping that someday we'll be able to be friends again. After all, we had twenty-two years and two wonderful kids together."

Marcia was silent again. I wondered how she would react to this "new" me.

Marcia took a deep breath and smiled. "Yeah, that's true, and they *are* great kids." We both sat silently as we thought about our 21 year-old daughter and 19 year-old son. It felt really good to share a moment of feeling like proud parents together. The warm nostalgia lingered on in quiet for what seemed like a long time. Neither of us wanted to break the heart warming silence with the interruption of words. Finally, in what amounted to almost a whisper, I asked, "So on this beautiful day, what would you like to talk about?"

Marcia laughed nervously. She looked away, then began almost apologetically, "Oh it's going to sound ridiculous now. You never responded to my lawyer's letter about returning my DVD collection, so I wanted to talk to you about it in person."

I could feel the first twinge of defensiveness pop up. We had been "arguing" for nearly a year over exactly who had ownership rites to the extensive movie collection we had created *together*. I knew it was a key moment. Happy seemed to be studying me—sending love out her eyes in hopes I would choose the high road.

I felt a wave of anger hit me. Instead of giving words to the feeling, I let the anger pass through me like clouds floating through an empty sky. I took a deep breath. To my amazement, I let out a spontaneous chuckle. The whole absurdity of arguing over our DVD collection hit me at once. After all, in the age of streaming videos, our 500 DVD movie collection wasn't even worth anything anymore. I began laughing. At first, it was more like a giggle, but it soon turned into a full-blown out of control belly laugh. Watching me laugh uncontrollably triggered Marcia to begin laughing as well. The ludicrousness of arguing about a worthless DVD collection must have hit her too. Before long,

Happy began barking excitedly in time with our laughing. Marcia and I were soon lying on our backs bellied over on the grass. Happy quickly traveled back and forth between the two of us, licking both our faces and barking her enthusiasm.

When we finally caught our breath and the laughing subsided, I managed to say, "How about we split the DVD's?"

Marcia, still breathing hard from our laughing, nodded agreeably. "That sounds like a great idea..." Then, as she slowly stood up, said, "Say, you wanna get a cup of coffee and get caught up with each other's lives? We could go to the Starbucks with the outside patio for Happy just a few blocks from here."

I looked up at Marcia while still sitting on the ground. I smiled in bewilderment at what had just taken place. "Sounds great."

As Marcia, my love guru, and I ambled towards Starbucks, I took note of the results of Happy's "experiment." It would seem that a potentially problematic disagreement had been turned into a love fest with a simple shift of attitude. This first lesson in the power of forgiveness and love would serve me well as I soon would face new and unexpected challenges.

While Marcia and I meandered towards the Starbucks, I could hear Happy's voice in my head: "You see! You see! Love works! It works! Just keep on loving Master Mark. You've been a *good boy*. You've been a very good boy!"

CHAPTER THREE

Let Sleeping Dogs Lie

"**H**appy, does anyone give you trouble?" I wondered out loud to my perpetually loving little girl.

"What do you mean, Master Mark?" she replied with real curiosity.

The conversation started while Happy and I were getting ready for bed. We both thought of the bed as "my bed," so we went through a nightly ritual of jockeying for who would get to sleep in the middle of the mattress. She generally lost that battle at night, but by morning, I often awoke to find myself hanging on to the side of the bed while she was sprawled out in the middle. She could be a very persistent little girl.

I further explained my question. "I mean, you seem so enthusiastic to see everyone that I wonder if you find it hard to be around certain individuals."

Happy gave me a look of love and empathy. She finally replied, "I was sometimes afraid to be around my previous Master, but that seems different than what you're talking about. Us dogs don't seem to stay upset at people for long periods of time like you humans do."

I had always wondered about this. Why do people sometimes hold grudges for years, or even decades, and dogs don't? I decided to directly ask Happy about it. "So, how the heck do you manage to not hold a grudge when someone mistreats you?"

I was now under the covers, with my body firmly in the middle of the bed. Happy stood by my feet, surveying the situation. We often had a little talk right before we turned off the lights. Happy let my question hang while she circled to find her perfect spot-- as close to the middle of the mattress as possible.

"I don't know how to hold a grudge," Happy began. "How do *you* manage to stay upset at people even when they're not around you?" she asked innocently.

Happy had a way of always turning my questions around so that I could look at myself anew. "That's a good question," I admitted. But before we go exploring how people manage to be so neurotic, I'd like to understand how *you* manage to be so forgiving. Maybe I could better understand how you don't hold grudges if you told me more about how it was for you with your previous owner."

I knew that Happy's previous owner, a man she called "Master Jerry," had somehow been responsible for her hurt back leg. I didn't know the whole story. I wondered if I would see any remnants of anger as I brought up the subject of her troubled past.

"Master Jerry was basically a good man," she began. He had a good heart when he wasn't drunk. When he would hit me, it wasn't really *him* that wanted to hurt me. It was the stuff he was drinking that made him act that way."

I thought about what she said for a moment before trying to summarize her philosophy. "So you're saying he wasn't really responsible for his actions because he was under the influence of a substance. You differentiate his actions while drunk from who he was when sober. Therefore, you don't hold a grudge against him since, without the alcohol, he was in your opinion a good man."

Happy tried to follow what I was saying. Finally she said, "That's a lot of words to explain something simple."

She'd say that whenever I made something that was really unpretentious into something that, to her, seemed convoluted and overly complex.

"It's really simple," she continued. I loved Master Jerry when he was nice; I was afraid of him when he was drunk. Why would I be angry with him now?"

I guess I could have come up with an answer to her question. I could have explained it would be "natural" to be upset at someone who mistreats you. I could have explained that some human beings would forever hold on to their past grievances with someone—even if the person that abused them had an "excuse" for their actions. But I didn't say anything. Her question, "Why would I be angry with him now?" stopped me in my tracks. It showed a level of forgiveness that was hard for me to even comprehend. I looked at her loving eyes and silently asked her, "How do you let such hurt go?"

Happy looked up at me from her comfortable position by my feet. "I don't know," she began. "That's just what dogs do; we let things go. We just shake it off—like how we shake water off ourselves after a bath. I was certainly afraid of Master Jerry when he was drunk, but why would I be afraid or angry when he was caring or playful?"

As often happened, Happy would say something from her point of view that would pull the carpet out from under *my* world view. All of a sudden, it seemed ridiculous to hold grievances towards a person who did something hurtful in the distant past. After all, whatever they did wasn't happening now—so what good would it do to focus on something in the past? Happy didn't have to "let things go," or even "forgive" her previous owner. She just managed to be with the *actual* person and behavior right in front of her. I thought to myself, "If only I could live in such a world."

"You *do* live in such a world," was Happy's reply to my thoughts. Her words in my head woke me up from my mental reverie. She continued, "You don't have to work through past problems with people; you don't have to *solve* problems at all. Problems can simply disappear with a fun game of chase or a bunch of loving licks. Once you're having a good time with someone, what's there to solve?"

Within a couple of months, I would learn that Happy was right about this. Having a "good time" with someone could be like a magical elixir to solve any problem. Unfortunately, I was not a quick student. Instead of learning this right away, I had to first bang my head against a few walls.

Happy's wisdom reminded me of how my ex-wife Marcia and I would engage in fruitless problem solving sessions that would last for hours. Like two prosecuting attorneys, we would square off at our kitchen table. We'd each lay down evidence as to how the other person was responsible for the various problems at hand. Secretly, we both hoped that upon hearing the evidence against them, our mate would say something like, "Yes, I now *see* that you're right! I've been wrong all this time and couldn't really see it till now. Thank you *so* much for showing me the errors of my ways!" Of course, such words were never spoken in our 22 years of marriage. Our trying to solve our problems by presenting our "cases" was a complete waste of time.

☆　　☆　　☆

Jerry Lester quickly stood up once the female AA speaker was done. Being six foot three, two hundred fifty pounds, he drew unwanted attention as he pulled up from his chair. Before any of his new AA buddies could ask him how he was doing, Jerry was out the door. He missed the nightly highs of alcohol intoxication. He missed going to the local bar. But most of all he missed his little Golden dog, Greta. On top of the longing for Greta and alcohol, Jerry also felt the guilt that came from knowing it was all his fault.

While driving back to his little condo, Jerry had an idea that electrified his heart like a bolt of lightning. "What if I could find Greta and get her back again?" The thought led to a surge of hope and adrenaline that coursed through his body. "Why didn't I think of that before?" he wondered to himself. Then he knew. Downing a pint of whiskey a day was not exactly the path to enlightened problem solving. Fortunately, he had some hope that those days were now behind him.

Jerry saw the exit to Corey Rd was only a mile up ahead. He knew there was some kind of animal shelter a couple of miles off that exit. He also knew that his driving privileges were only to AA meetings and his job. But he couldn't wait. Jerry tracked down the Humane Society shelter like a man on a mission. Once he found the building, he parked his car and practically jogged to the front office.

Jerry quickly spotted the elderly gentleman behind the counter. He blurted out, "My name is Jerry Lester and I lost my dog about three months ago. She looked like a little Golden Retriever. I'm here to see if you have any record of her being picked up."

The gray haired man eyed Jerry suspiciously. "Three months ago. That's an awfully long time to wait before checkin' on your dog."

Jerry's mind raced to come up with some reasonable story, but nothing surfaced. After a few seconds, he sighed. "I'll level with you sir. I'm one month sober. The two months after I lost Greta are kind of a blur, but I really loved that dog. Now that I'm sober and going to meetings, I feel like I could really take care of her properly."

The elderly man looked deep into Jerry's eyes—trying to get a sense of the man. After what seemed like a long time, he said, "Yeah, I think I remember the one you're talking about. She was a real cutie—and smart. But she was picked up by someone about a month after she arrived. I'm sorry, but I can't give out information as to her new owner. For that, you would have to get a court order."

*   *   *

After I had asked Happy a bunch of questions, I was convinced she really didn't have any hard feelings towards her previous owner. It was hard to imagine her loyalty—considering that she was subjected to occasional drunken beatings. Then why did she escape from him, and how did she end up at the shelter? I needed to know. I hesitantly decided to ask. "Happy, if you loved Jerry, then why did you escape from him?"

Happy was quiet for a long moment. She looked sad. When her eyes caught mine, they looked droopy, like the wind had been knocked out of her. Between her expressive eyes and her ever-moving ears, it was always easy to know exactly what she was feeling. Finally she said, "I didn't escape from him. He was taken from me. It was horrible. It was really hard. I still have nightmares about it. I hope he got the help he needed." Happy breathed a big sigh. Though still curled up in a ball, she lifted her head and shook it quickly back and forth—like trying to shake off a bug on her head. Finally, she continued, "But now I'm grateful for all that happened. Without that difficult time, I never would have found you. I guess it was all part of love's big plan."

I didn't know exactly what she meant, but I appreciated her philosophy. However, rather than ask her about her philosophy, I still wanted to know about how she ended up at the shelter. I felt hesitant to ask her something that would likely bring up a traumatic memory, but I felt I had to know. Delicately, I said to Happy, "Would you be willing to tell me how you ended up in the shelter?"

There was dead silence for what seemed like an eternity. Finally, I heard her say, "If you must know, it would be better for me to show you. Words are not very good for describing some things. I bet you can't really describe in words the sadness you felt when Marcia left you. I can't really explain in words the hardship that led me to the shelter. Dogs tend to 'think' in pictures. But if you want to know how I ended up in a shelter, I will try to show you in pictures. These pictures are forever in my head, and maybe by sharing them with you, you'll learn something that will be of help to you."

I felt honored by Happy's trust in me. I quickly realized she was going to share a traumatic memory with me, as well as an ability I didn't know she had. Evidently, Happy could not only share her thoughts with me, but also her mental pictures. She instructed me to close my eyes and relax. I took some deep breaths, not knowing exactly what to expect. The next thing I remember was seeing a clear image in my mind of Jerry coming home drunk and seeing pee on the kitchen floor. I was seeing this "brain picture" as if from Happy's viewpoint. From her perspective, Jerry was like an elephant who towered over her. I could feel that Happy both cared for this big man and was afraid for her life. The next picture was of Jerry screaming at her. Then she saw Jerry pick up a portable fire extinguisher near the stove and, in a fit of rage, hurl it in her direction. I was aghast.

Happy was right—words could not explain what I saw and felt next. Perhaps the best way I can describe it would be to imagine being a defenseless baby and having your angry mother deliberately smash your leg with a baseball bat. That's the kind of all encompassing pain I got from her "transmission" to me. When the fire extinguisher hit her back leg, her leg and heart were both broken. She couldn't move, and Happy thought Jerry might try to kill her. She was paralyzed with fear and yelping in pain. She tried to run away, but her legs failed her. I wanted to reach out and hold my little girl, and stop this horrible movie from getting any worse.

The next picture Happy showed me was of Jerry bending over her, softly weeping and lightly petting the top of her head. She was still crying, but now she knew she wouldn't be beaten. Evidently, her fear and yelps of pain yanked Jerry out of his drunken rage.

Jerry gently picked Happy up in his arms and, as she whimpered softly, carried her into the cab of his flatbed truck. Then he sped off—apparently to get her some help.

The ensuing image I saw was that of Happy seeing flashing red lights behind the truck. Happy looked up at Jerry who was hitting the steering wheel with both hands while screaming. Jerry slowly pulled the truck over to the side of the road and stopped his vehicle. A cop soon appeared at his window, and Jerry was asked to step outside. For an awfully long while, Happy sat in the front seat of the truck, utterly alone, scared, and in great physical pain. She began to shiver uncontrollably.

Then the most wrenching image of all appeared in my mind. Jerry, now in handcuffs, was given a few moments to say goodbye to his one friend and loving companion. He opened the door to his cab and spotted his little girl curled up, shivering, and crying softly. With both hands held together by the handcuffs, Jerry awkwardly tried to stroke and soothe his beloved pet. Happy was whimpering softly, trying to understand what was happening.

Jerry's tears fell on top of Happy's head. She and Jerry both sensed this was going to be the last time they would ever see each other. Her heart was racing, but her searing pain kept her from sitting up and licking Jerry's tears away. When his hands approached her face, she licked his bound hands as best she could. Jerry positioned himself so he could look in his little girl's eyes. When their eyes met, he mumbled, "I'm so sorry, I'm so sorry." Between his sobs, Jerry repeated, "Please forgive me... I love you so much. I love you so much."

Happy nuzzled her nose into Jerry's bound hands and licked his fingers as best she could. She could taste his tears amidst the smell of sweat and alcohol. She wanted Jerry to know that she still loved him. Then, Happy heard the cop say to Jerry, "Okay, bud, time to go. Come on."

Happy saw Jerry being pulled away by the man in the black uniform. Jerry's hands reached out to touch Happy one last time, but the officer over powered him and his hands could no longer reach her. As the door of the cab closed with a thud, Happy heard Jerry say through the window, "You're such a good girl. I love you so much." And then he was gone.

Happy was utterly alone in the pick up truck. She was cold, she was frightened, and her back leg hurt very badly. Time passed slowly. She shivered uncontrollably. She whimpered, but there was no one to hear her cries. She lay there alone for what seemed like an eternity. She cried silently to herself. There was absolutely nothing she could do. Finally, after a long while, another man in a black uniform opened the door of the pick up truck. Upon seeing Happy alone in the truck, the young man said in a gentle voice, "Are you scared little one? Let me see if I can help you?" Gently, slowly, the man tenderly carried her into his waiting car.

The final picture Happy showed me was of being carried into the animal shelter office by the young man who had found her in Jerry's car. A woman in a white uniform examined her leg, and then she put a very big needle into her hip area. That's the last picture Happy gave me.

By now, I had a tear rolling down my cheek. I slowly opened my eyes, and when I was ready, I met Happy's eyes with my own. I sensed she needed to know I understood the pain she had been through. I held her head in my left hand and softly stroked the top of her head with my right hand. I said, "Oh sweetie, you poor little girl. That must have been so painful. You don't have to be frightened any more. I won't ever leave you. I will always be here for you."

Happy soaked up my love and empathy like a sponge. It felt wonderful to have my love so fully received by her. After all she had done for me, it felt uniquely satisfying to be able to give back to her in this way.

Once Happy and I felt done with our loving embrace, she looked up at me with her soft brown eyes and said, "But all that's in the past. I'm a Happy girl now that I'm with you. Before I met you my name was Greta, but once I met you, I really became Happy." Then, my little pooch stood up and moved to the center of the room. She stretched into a "downward dog" yoga pose, then abruptly shook her entire body as if shaking excess water off after a bath. Once the shaking was complete, she seemed back to her normal, cheerful self. It was quite a transformation.

Happy quickly walked across the room and began gnawing on an old tennis ball. She seemed quite content. I thought to myself that I needed to try that shaking routine sometime. Then I remembered there was a popular song on the radio by Taylor Swift that was about shaking. I hummed a few bars in my head so the lyrics would come back to me. Soon, I had reached the chorus:

"...Cause the players gonna play...
And the haters gonna hate...
Heart breakers gonna break...
And the fakers gonna fake...
Baby, I'm just gonna shake...
I shake it off, I shake it off."

Hidden within a catchy pop tune was a lot of wisdom. People are gonna do what they do, but as Happy had so recently demonstrated, it's possible to simply "shake it off." I thought to myself,

"What if every time I was lost in a dramatic story in my head, I could simply shake my whole body and quickly be done with it?" Note to self: next time you' re feeling depressed or anxious, try shaking it off. I hoped that gnawing on an old tennis ball afterwards was optional for making this method so effective.

CHAPTER 4

A Dog Eat Dog World

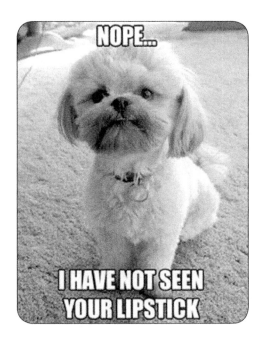

I remember the day clearly. It was really just like any other day. Little did I know that a simple letter delivered from the mailman would soon send me into a tailspin. As I opened up the letter from the Humane Society, I wondered what this could possibly be about. When I began reading the words, my heart sank. A flood of emotions poured through my body. The letter read:

Dear Mr. Moseley,

We regret to inform you that the previous owner of your Golden mix female has made a claim on this dog. If a claim is made on a dog from a previous owner within the first 120 days of adoption, we are required by law to bring the matter before a judge for consideration. A court date has been set for you and the previous owner, Jerry Lester, to appear at the 11th Superior Court in Los Angeles California on June 17th of this year at 10 am. If this time can not work for you, please call our office at 310-292-3072 and we will arrange another time.

Thank you for your help in this matter.

Sincerely,
Robert Blum,
Humane Society Legal Affairs

I immediately went into panic mode. I hid the letter in my desk. Maybe if it was out of sight it would be out of mind. It only took a few seconds to see that such an action wasn't going to help. Although at the time I had known Happy for just four months, it felt more like four years. She was my lifeline. Losing her would have been like losing access to oxygen. My mind went into overdrive. I thought of hiring a lawyer; I thought of hiring a hit man to get rid of Jerry Lester; I thought of moving to another state. I was quickly losing control.

I knew I needed to talk to someone who would understand my feelings, and yet not be thrown for a loop the way that I was. I decided to call Marcia. I nervously picked up my cell and started dialing.

"Hello?" she answered. It feel good to hear her voice.

"Hi Marcia, " I quickly began, "Something has come up, and I didn't know who to turn to. Do you have a couple of minutes?"

"Sure, what's up? Is everything all right?" she sounded truly worried.

"No it isn't," I replied. "I just got a letter from the Humane Society and it says that Happy's previous owner has made a claim on her." I could hear my voice sounded like that of a man in the midst of a panic attack. "It says I need to appear in court on June 17th to decide who gets to keep her."

"Oh my. Oh my. I'm so sorry Mark. I really am." There was a long silence before Marcia spoke again. "Have you thought of hiring a lawyer?"

"No, but I've thought of hiring a hit man—does that count?" I said, allowing some humor to enter into the conversation.

Marcia chuckled awkwardly. "That might not be the best idea. Besides, a lawyer is a bit like a hit man—only legal." Our quick entrance into witty banter reminded me of how we used to sometimes use humor as a defense against stressful times.

I took a slow deep breath. "Yeah, a lawyer sounds like a good idea. Shit. I didn't need this now. I can't lose my little girl."

"I'm sure it'll all work out," Marcia said reassuringly.

Without thinking, I replied "You sound like Happy."

"What do you mean I sound like Happy?" Marcia asked suspiciously.

I had forgotten that Marcia was not having the same conversations with Happy that I was. To her, Happy was a cute, loving dog. To me, Happy was my therapist, pal, and guru all rolled up into one furry package. I stammered, "I mean you both tend to look on the bright side of things."

"Oh," Marcia said. "Well sometimes that's what's needed."

"Yeah, I guess so," I said half-heartedly. "Well, thanks. I guess hiring a lawyer is probably a good idea."

I didn't want to overstay my welcome with Marcia, and I didn't know what else to say. After all, it was already pretty awkward calling up your ex when you've been separated for over a year. I thanked Marcia for her advice and hung up the phone. Then I stepped out of my office and into the piercing eyes of my little Golden girl. I hadn't thought of what to tell Happy, but when I saw her, I immediately averted her gaze.

"What's wrong?" she asked. She could sense my emotions better than I could.

"Nothing," I stammered. Then thinking she'd know that was a total lie, I continued, "I just got a disturbing letter from the IRS. It ends up I owe them some money."

"Well, Master Mark, I can't help you with that. I don't really get why collecting green pieces of paper with dead people on it is so important—no matter how many times you try to explain it to me."

Happy's view of how ridiculous human undertakings seemed to her always hit me like a cold slap in the face. All I could say in response was, "Well, my pooch, we live in different worlds."

"Yes," she agreed. They're different, but I know what hiding a trauma feels like, and that never feels good. I feel much better now that I know you understand my history with my previous Master. But somehow I smell that you're very afraid. Is there something else bothering you?"

I was never a very good liar, and Happy could smell deception almost as well as a new dog in the neighborhood.

"Why do you ask?" I responded, trying to look casual while knowing she could sense something was off.

"Well, you smell really afraid. If there's something you're not telling me, maybe you'd feel better if you told me."

Happy looked at me with her eyes of unconditional love, but I was doing my best to resist her charms.

"You know," Happy began, "not telling the truth creates a wall that keeps love out. It looks like you could use some love now. I know you're frightened. When you're afraid, that's when you need love the most. Please tell me...why are you so fearful?"

I still wasn't convinced it was a good idea to tell Happy about the letter. My mind made up the story that it would just make her upset. Besides, there was certainly nothing she could do about it—so why tell her? It's funny how my mind could always come up with a quick excuse to not open up to those that I loved. Marcia certainly knew that tendency in me, and now it was interfering with my connection to Happy. Same old obstacles to love, just this time with a new species.

Unlike Marcia, Happy knew just what to do in such a situation. Instead of insisting I tell her the truth, she just came up and started licking my hand. Then she licked my face. I didn't hear any of her thoughts telling me what I needed to do. No lectures on how I should be different. No angry growls or looks of hurt. Just love. After a minute or two of her pure devotion, I broke down. Tears streamed down from my face. I could no longer hide what was going on with me.

"Oh Happy, I'm so scared. I just got a letter from the Humane Society saying that your old owner, Jerry, wants you back. The law states that he can make a claim on you if I've had you for less than four months. I don't know what I'd do if I lost you girl."

Happy listened attentively. Then, she licked up the tears as they fell from my face. She always knew just the right thing to do to make me feel better.

"Thank you for telling me Master Mark," she began. It's always better when we share hard news with those we love. I'm sure it will all work out okay in the end."

I appreciated Happy's love. It felt good to have my wall of separation and lies crumble in the face of her adoration. It felt good to share my burden. However, her Pollyanna platitudes were, in my opinion, not exactly the help I needed. I needed to call a lawyer. I expressed as much to her.

"I don't know what a lawyer is," was her response, "but I do know the most important thing is you need to have faith that it will all work out if you love enough."

Happy's words hit me the wrong way. "That's naïve," I objected. "We live in a dog eat dog world. There are winners and there are losers, and if I don't hire a lawyer to go after this guy, I could lose you."

"First of all, dogs don't eat other dogs," Happy protested. "Most dogs lead with love, and they have faith that if they love first, others will love them back. You should learn from them."

The combination of Happy's unconditional love followed by her words of straight up truth felt like a one-two punch to my gut. I found myself creating a wall of protection. Then, I got defensive. "You're a dog. It's different in the human world. In the world of people, there are folks who will try to hurt you. There are folks who will deceive you, or take you to court to get what is rightfully yours."

Happy fell silent as she looked at me worriedly. After a quick sneeze and a thorough shaking of her body to clear her mood, she began, "All I know is that love works. Love is the most powerful force in the world. When you put your faith in the power of love, good things happen. Maybe not right away, but in the end it always works out."

I begrudgingly listened to Happy's short sermon. I still thought she was being naïve. Yet, I felt safe enough with her to hear her out and try to work through our differences. I knew that even if we disagreed, she'd still love me. Maybe she was right. Love was certainly a healing tonic.

"Yes, love is a powerful force," I admitted, "but you don't know about lawyers and courts and people who lie."

"You're right, I don't," she said softly. "But I know things that you don't. I know there's a soft spot in even the meanest junkyard dog—and I assume it's the same with people. I know that love opens up a world of miracles. I don't understand it all. I just know that it works."

I could sense that Happy felt she was on solid ground. I was not going to get her to budge from her position. She was so sure of the power of love that it began making me question my own beliefs. I started feeling a little shaky. I had been so sure I was right just a few moments ago. It reminded me of something I had heard from a self-help guru on TV. He said that our belief systems are simply a bunch of B.S. They're not the truth, they're just **b**elief **s**ystems. I wondered if I was being run by a belief system that my parents had instilled in me.

Happy sensed a little opening in me. "Well, Master Mark, you should do whatever you feel is best. But whatever you do, do it with love in your heart."

Although well intentioned, Happy's words sounded like something from a poster from the 1960's. Make love, not war. Give peace a chance. Turn the other cheek. Yeah, right. That didn't work out so well for Jesus. I realized that, for me, things were either black or white. You either love someone, or you make them your enemy. You're either a doormat or the victor. Her philosophy was maybe good for church, but it could never stand up in the real world.

I thought of Jerry--her former owner. I could never "love" someone who beat my pure, innocent girl. Just thinking of him made my blood boil. And now he was trying to steal my little girl from me. What an asshole! What nerve this guy had. If I didn't take down this jerk, he'd destroy Happy. He'd destroy me. I imagined taking this turkey apart with my bear hands.

"Are you done?" Happy asked, snapping me back from my self-righteous fantasy.

"What are you saying?" I asked. Her interruption of my fantasy jarred me.

"I'm wondering if you're done with your dream?" asked Happy, her eyes as loving as always.

"I guess so." I didn't know how to answer that. What was she getting at?

Happy saw my confusion so she continued. "I have noticed that humans like to make up bad dreams in their head. I just don't get it. Why spend time making up scary dreams?"

Her question was like another slap in the face. I thought about her question for a moment—realizing I didn't have a really good answer. Finally, I blurted out, "Well sometimes bad things happen in the world, and you need to be prepared for the worst case scenario."

"So imagining bad things will make things better?" she asked.

Happy asked the question with such innocence that, instead of getting defensive, I realized how absurd it sounded. But I was not going to give in so easily. "Yes, sometimes imagining what you call 'bad dreams' can help to prevent such things from happening."

Happy looked confused. She tilted her head in her classic look of trying to figure out something slightly beyond her comprehension. "But if you imagine these bad things over and over again, won't that make it *more* likely the bad dreams will come true?"

I realized that maybe she had a point, but I was no longer in search of the truth. After all, I had a belief system to protect—even if it was something that had been passed down from my parents. I countered, "So you think everyone should just think positive thoughts all day? That didn't work out so well when Jerry would beat you." I realized I was "hitting" her with a low blow, but nothing was going to stop me from making my point.

Happy waited a long while to respond. She'd do this whenever she felt like I wasn't listening. It was her way of rebooting my system. Finally, she began, "All I know is that one growl leads to another. Soon, everyone is showing their teeth and nothing good happens. Leading with love is the only way that things get better."

Happy had a way of saying things in a simple manner that made my arguments sound pretty stupid. Sometimes it really pissed me off. My patience was running out. I decided to play the "Master" card.

"Look Happy, I'm the Master and you're the dog." My tone of voice indicated that I was beginning a self-righteous rant. "I have more experience than you. Maybe your ideas work for a dog, but they don't work in the real world of people. I need to hire a lawyer and I'm going to have to battle this out with your former owner. I'm sorry if this bothers you, but that's just the way it is. I'm not going to be anyone's doormat."

There was another long silence. It looked like Happy was searching for a way into my heart, but I had locked all the windows and doors. Finally, she began whimpering. This was *her* version of a "low blow." It was impossible to defend against a sad, lonely whimper.

"Don't try that on me," I managed to bellow. You're not going to change my mind. I'm hiring a lawyer."

"It's okay to hire a lawyer—whatever that is," she countered. I just don't like seeing you with a closed mind and a closed heart. You look so sad like that."

Another low blow I thought. This little girl knew all of my emotional buttons. It felt like the same old arguments I used to have with Marcia, but this bitch was even better at manipulating me. I threw up my hands. "Look. We're not getting anywhere with this argument. I'm hiring a lawyer and that's final. You should be thankful I'm willing to pay whatever is necessary to keep you from that monster."

Happy stared at me before responding. "He's not a monster," she replied softly in my head. "He's afraid—just like you."

Happy's words had a sobering effect on me. For the first time I realized that she still loved this man, this jerk. Now my fear of losing her became even more intense. I was now like a jealous lover lashing out. "He beat you for God's sakes! He's a monster! I'm not going to let your misguided loyalty lead us both into a catastrophe."

Happy just stared at me again, then whimpered a little as she slowly walked away. I felt like she had conceded the argument. I had won. I took a couple of slow breaths, savoring my victory. Yet, sitting there alone, the sweet taste of victory began to sour. I still had to deal with the letter. But now, in addition, my Golden girl thought I was being an idiot. She was right. With my heart and mind all closed down and defended, I did feel sad. Very sad.

I pulled out my iPhone from my pocket and called my lawyer, Steve. He was the guy who was handling the divorce papers for Marcia and I. I didn't know if Steve would have any experience in a case like this, but I didn't know who else to call. Steve's voicemail picked up and I briefly explained the situation and read him the letter. Steve would know what to do. He was smart and tough. At $300 an hour, he better be. I put down the phone. I felt empty. I worried about what would happen next.

CHAPTER 5

Barking Up the Wrong Tree

I get a lot of calls during the day. Of course, there are always clients asking me tax questions. Then there's the endless stream of telemarketers. If I see a call is from out of state and they're not in my contact list, I never answer it. When I heard my iPhone ring on this particular morning, I didn't recognize the number that showed up. However, it was from my same area code, so I answered it. As is my usual way of answering calls, I immediately put it on speaker phone. Big mistake.

"Hi, this is Mark," I said in my automatic phone answering voice.

At first there was silence. Perhaps they thought it was my voicemail answering. But then a slightly gravely voice said, "Hi Mark, this is Jerry Lester. I was Greta's former owner."

My heart immediately began racing. My mind soon joined in on the race. I thought of hanging up, but quickly thought better about it. After all, Happy was already listening in, and I knew she would be very unhappy with such behavior. "Okay," I heard myself say hesitatingly. "Why are you calling?"

"Well, I'm in AA now, and part of my twelve step program is to make amends for errors I have made. I'm calling you to say I apologize for taking this case to court. I know that must be hard on you."

I felt my blood boil. I wanted to punch something, but there was nothing nearby to take my anger out on. "Hard? " I shouted into the phone. "You have no idea!" I was immediately in full reactive mode. The fact that Happy was in the room and listening in was no longer in my awareness. I felt like a rabid dog just wanting to take a bite out of this guy.

Jerry quickly interrupted, "Wait, just please calm down a moment and let me explain myself."

I quickly interrupted him. "*My* dog has already told me everything I need to know about you," I started... "How you abused her, how you threw a god damn fire extinguisher at her. There's no way you're going to take my dog away from me!"

"How'd you know about the fire extinguisher?" Jerry responded, sounding both surprised and confused.

I realized that trying to answer his question would only open up a can of worms, so I ignored it. "Her back leg is still hurting her to this day. You should have been arrested for what you did!"

"I *was* arrested" Jerry said, raising his voice. "I was charged with drunk driving. And I didn't abandon her; I was taken away from her in handcuffs. There was nothing I could do. It was horrible!"

I was not going to let this guy off so easily. Although his words registered in my mind, the momentum of my anger pushed me forward to respond. "You could have not beaten her; you could have given her a damn collar and tag, you could have not left her to die in a cage for a month." I was on a roll. Admittedly it felt good to express my self-righteous rant.

I heard a loud sigh on the other end of the phone. I could hear him taking a couple of slow, deep breaths. Finally, Jerry began to speak in a measured voice. "First, I don't want to make excuses for being a drunk. But you should know I'm two months sober now. Second, I was in *jail* for six weeks due to a previous DUI, so I couldn't exactly take her home. And finally, I took her collar off deliberately the night she got hurt because I thought it was bothering her. That's why she had no tag."

Jerry's words were like a monkey wrench in my anger generating mind machine. To my chagrin, some part of my brain realized this guy was sounding almost reasonable, but I was in no mood for forgiveness. Having repeatedly played the images of Happy being beaten up by this jerk, I was not going to let go of my anger in a flash.

I spat out the words, "Well, she's my dog now, and she's very happy. In fact, that's her name now—Happy. The next time I plan to talk to you Mr. Lester is when I see you in court. You get what I'm saying?"

"I hear you," Jerry responded meekly.

There was nothing else to say, so I hung up the phone. I felt like I had told him off, and that felt good. Unfortunately, sitting obediently nearby was Happy staring at me with her penetrating, sad eyes.

I turned to face her. I was angry. "What?" I shouted. "Why are you looking at me like that? I'm not gonna let the man who beat you steal you away from me. And you're not gonna make me feel guilty about yelling at him." I could feel my defensiveness rising up with each word I said. On the other hand, without saying a single word in my head, Happy had a way of getting her point across with just a simple look.

Finally, Happy's words streamed into my mind. "I think you're barking up the wrong tree."

Happy had a way of getting through to me that Marcia, in twenty-two years of marriage, never managed to equal. She'd give me "the look" with her penetrating eyes, then whimper or say a single sentence that was impossible to defend against.

She had me hooked. Reluctantly I asked Happy, "What do you mean you think I'm barking up the wrong tree?"

Happy's demeanor was patient, like she was talking to a slightly slow child. "Well, you're thinking that taking the low road instead of the high road will get you what you want. To me that looks like you're barking up the wrong tree."

I felt defensive. It's never easy taking feedback from someone you love. "What makes you think I'm taking the low road? I'm trying to save you from a life of being abused."

Happy shook her head. "Maybe you need me to explain what I mean by low road and high road. You don't seem to understand."

Although Happy's thoughts struck me as condescending, they were said in a totally loving manner. In a somewhat snarky tone of voice I responded, "Well maybe you can explain it to me."

Happy slowly led me from my office to the living room. Once there, she jumped up on the couch, and with her eyes invited me to have a seat next to her. I obliged. Even when I got angry at her,

I couldn't stay annoyed for long. One look at her endearing face, and the defenses around my heart would begin to melt.

Finally we were both comfortably ensconced on the couch. "Did you ever see the movie 'The Matrix?'" she asked, her eyes sparkling with interest.

Asking about a movie was not the approach I thought she'd use to show me the errors of my ways. Happy had a way of throwing me curveballs like this—especially when she knew I'd be too well defended to hear any rational argument. "No," I admitted. "I never saw that movie. Why are you asking me about it?" I said impatiently.

"Master Jerry and I watched it several times," she started. "It's one of my favorites. There's a part in the movie where the hero is asked if he wants to take a red pill or a blue pill. The red pill represents taking the high road and learning the truth; the blue pill represents taking the low road and avoiding the truth. I think life gets better and better when you take the red pill—the high road. But today with Master Jerry, it looks to me like you took the low road."

I reacted protectively. "I don't see how confronting him with his abusive past is taking the low road." As I said my words, I didn't fully believe them. I had done more than remind Jerry about his past. I had tried to hurt him. I figured that probably was not the high road.

"Being self righteous and angry is easy," Happy began. "That's the low road; the blue pill. Being forgiving and vulnerable and honest about your own weaknesses—that's the red pill. That's the high road."

Somewhere in me I knew that Happy was right, but my ego was not going to give in so easily. "So you think we should always be forgiving, and let people be abusive, and all just sing Kumbahya together?"

Happy gave me a slow look of disappointment. "Your reply is a good example of taking the blue pill. It was a little way of taking the low road by being sarcastic instead of trying to understand. Taking the red pill in *that* moment would have been to try to understand what I was saying. Instead, you simply made fun of what I said. We always have a choice between taking the red pill or the blue pill with each new moment."

I felt cornered. Between Happy's disarming eyes and her philosophical chops, I knew I could never win an argument with her. I decided to give up even trying, and instead explore this red pill/blue pill concept with her. I took a couple of slow deep breaths. Then, in an effort to try to be sincere, I asked Happy, "So do you think we should always take the red pill?"

"Yippee, you did it. You just took a little red pill," Happy excitedly responded.

Seeing Happy smile with her eyes brightened up my mood. "What are you talking about you zany mutt?" I often called her a zany mutt when she expressed excitement for reasons I was at a loss to understand.

"You stopped being a growly bear and instead asked a question that showed a desire for real learning. That's taking a little red pill," she explained.

"But it was only a simple question," I found myself being argumentative again. How is *that* taking a red pill? Isn't taking the red pill a little dangerous?"

Happy's tail wagged feverishly. She was excited that I had began exploring an idea *with* her—rather than just argue with her. "It can be dangerous," Happy responded, "but most the time it's just a little bit hard. Most of life is not about the danger of crossing a busy street. Instead, it's about the little choices we make such as not being a growly bear, or choosing to be kind, or trying to be honest or vulnerable."

From Happy's explanation I could see that she was right; I had just taken a little red pill. I had let go of having to be right, and instead began exploring an idea with my little girl. It was not such an easy thing to do.

Happy interrupted my self-congratulations. "You deserve to celebrate," she said. "It may seem like a small step, but that's what life is—a series of small steps. How many times a day do you take the high road versus the low road?"

I smiled sheepishly. "Do I have to answer that?" We both knew the answer was almost never. Until Happy had brought it up, I didn't even think in terms of 'taking the high road.' I confessed to Happy, "Well now I feel guilty that I took the low road, or what you call the blue pill with Jerry."

Happy looked me over just to make sure I was being sincere. After a moment, she responded forgivingly. "There's always another moment ahead, and always another chance to take the high road."

Just then, we both heard a knock at the door. Happy joyfully ran to see who it was. I had the humorous thought that I wondered why dogs always run to the door when someone knocks. After all, it's hardly ever for them!

I opened the door and was surprised to see it was Marcia. Happy, of course, went crazy. She started squealing in delight, licking any part of Marcia she could lick. Then, Happy quickly ran into the living room, grabbed a stuffed toy, brought it to Marcia, and laid it at her feet as a sort of offering. Whoever came through the front door, whether it be me or someone she'd never met, Happy would go through a similar routine. I always got great enjoyment from watching the whole spectacle. It was endearing to witness any living being display so much enthusiasm.

Once Marcia and Happy's love reunion was coming to a close, Marcia looked up at me. I must have looked quite astonished to see her because she smiled nervously and said, "I hope it's alright that I stopped by unannounced. I was in the area, and I have some mail to drop off for you. Besides, it gives me a chance to say 'hello' to Happy."

It was good to see Marcia. However, her comment about mostly being there to see Happy stung a bit. I noticed I was slightly hurt that she wasn't there to check up on me since the distressing call I had made to her a couple of days prior. Strangely, after her comment and the little hurt I felt, time slowed down for me. It felt a little strange. In my mind, I imagined a little fork in the road before me. One fork in the road was a picture of me doing what I normally do—smile and let the comment pass. I suddenly knew *that* action would be taking the blue pill, the low road. Or I could reveal that I was a little hurt that Marcia wasn't there to see me. The red pill. Although it was only a little red pill, in that moment it seemed hard to swallow.

I heard myself say, "It's good to see you Marcia, although honestly, I'm a little hurt that you didn't come to say 'hi' to *me*." I was in new, red pill territory and it felt a little bit dangerous.

Marcia was taken aback by my remark. Happy, on the other hand had a nose for "red pill moments." She wagged her tail and came over to lick my hand. After a few seconds Marcia finally said, "I'm sorry Mark. Truthfully I came over to see you too, but I guess I couldn't say that straight out."

Now all three of us were in red pill territory. I didn't really know what would happen next. I suddenly realized how much of daily conversation was just mechanically filling up space and being polite. All blue pill territory. However, a single honest, vulnerable remark seemed to trigger a whole series of red pill moments. I didn't know exactly what to say in response to Marcia's apology, so I didn't say anything. Standing there silent in the entryway with my ex wife—just looking at each other—that seemed like another red pill moment.

Finally, I stammered, "I appreciate you saying that Marcia. You're a good red pill taker."

Marcia laughed nervously. "What are you talking about? What's a red pill taker?"

I shot a knowing glance to Happy, then asked Marcia, "You ever see the movie 'The Matrix?'"

"Sure. Wonderful movie."

"Well, remember the scene where the hero is asked if he wants to take a red pill or a blue pill?" I inquired.

"Yes, that's one of my favorite scenes." Marcia responded.

In another attempt at a red pill moment, I looked Marcia squarely in the eyes. "So I was just saying that you're pretty good at taking the high road, and being vulnerable and speaking your truth. Over the course of our marriage I often didn't like hearing the truth, but I commend you for your commitment to it."

It felt vulnerable to say such things to Marcia while our divorce papers were ready to get filed. I thought to myself that had I said such things while we were together, perhaps we would not even be getting a divorce.

Marcia interrupted my self-flagellation. "Well, that's wonderful to hear." Looking me in the eyes for a quiet moment, she continued, "I'm appreciating the changes I've been seeing in you Mark. Maybe getting a dog has been exactly what you've been needing all these years."

I tried to avoid dismissing her complement the way I normally might. I patted Happy on the head before responding, "Well I hired her to teach me how to express love and be happy, and she's been working overtime." I gave Happy a quick wink, then turned to Marcia, "Why don't you come in and I'll get you a cup of tea."

"I'd like that." Marcia walked over to the living room couch, and Happy followed enthusiastically behind. I walked into the kitchen and put a pot on the stove. The water was already warm, so in a couple of minutes, I brought over two cups of mint tea on a tray. As I brought the tea into the living room, Happy gave me a look suggesting, "What about me?" I didn't need to hear her words in my head—a simple look was enough. I went to the pantry and got Happy a biscuit. I told her to sit, which she did with quick obedience. Then I gave her the treat. I thought to myself, "If only I were as obedient in following Happy's directives as she is with me, maybe I'd get more 'treats' in life."

I sat down near Marcia on the couch. Happy swiftly jumped onto the couch between us. We both began petting her on opposite sides of her body. Marcia commented, "This little girl is getting a Happy love sandwich. Wherever there's love to be had, she seems to find the exact right place to soak it all up."

I wholeheartedly agreed. We both looked down adoringly at this four-legged little love sponge. After almost a year of dealing with divorce filing minutiae with Marcia, it felt strange to be sharing my love for Happy with her. It brought back memories of how Marcia and I always adored our kids together. Unfortunately, when the kids left the house, we suddenly found ourselves without any children to love together, and no more love between us. While Marcia and I were no longer in love, feeling mutual love for an adorable dog felt a bit like being in love. It felt good to have some of the hurts of separation wash away in that moment.

"So," I began, "How are you doing?" Evidently, I was back to my normal mode of superficial conversation.

"I'm doing well. And you?"

"I'm doing okay I guess," I heard myself reply.

After our red pill moments and mutual adoration of Happy, our shallow manner of greeting each other felt truly odd. Once again, I could envision a fork in the road of my future. On one side was the road of honesty, trust, and unpredictability. On the other fork was the banality of pleasantries and safety. Having been recently inspired, I chose the red pill again.

"Marcia, can I talk to you about something that came up this morning that really shook me up?"

Marcia sat up straight on the couch, giving me her full attention. "Of course Mark, what is it?" Marcia had always been a good listener. Unfortunately, during our marriage I hadn't been much of a talker.

"Well," I began, "as you know, a few days ago I got a letter from the Humane Society saying I need to appear in court regarding who gets to keep Happy."

"Yes, of course I remember that. Have you hired a lawyer like I suggested?"

"I did," I responded.

Unlike me, Marcia seemed to like and trust lawyers. During the past year, it seemed like I had received at least one letter each month from her attorney. They always left a bad taste in my mouth, but I tried to put those feelings aside for the moment.

"So," I started hesitatingly, "Happy's previous owner, a man named Jerry, actually called me this morning. Can you believe that?"

Marcia gasped. "I'm not even sure if that's legal."

I appreciated her reaction. "Legal or not, he did it. He said he's in AA now and was trying to make amends."

"Well, what did you say?" Marcia asked.

"Truthfully, I was pretty nasty to him. I told him there's no way in hell I'm gonna let a dog abuser take Happy away from me. Then I basically told him I'll see him in court and hung up." I looked up at Marcia to see how she was reacting to my account.

I wanted her to say something like, "Good for you," but that's not how she reacted. She changed her body position on the couch, took a deep breath then responded, "Did he seem like he was sincere? Was he really calling to make amends?"

Marcia's question to me made me feel uncomfortable. I realized I had not previously considered her question. I had been so reactive to hearing Jerry's voice that his level of sincerity never registered to me. But as I thought back to his words, I realized that he indeed did sound sincere. I confessed as much to Marcia, then asked her, "Do you think I did the right thing?"

When Marcia failed to give a quick reply, I knew her answer. Carefully she began, "Well, we've just spent the last year making an enemy out of each other, and that sure sucked. Even if you have to take someone to court, it doesn't do any good to turn them into an enemy."

"That's basically what Happy said," I shot back, then abruptly realized how absurd that would sound to Marcia. I quickly tried to cover my tracks by stating, "I mean, Happy's philosophy seems to be to never hold grudges and to love everyone." I felt my face get red and hoped that my reference to Happy's 'words' would not be questioned.

Marcia accepted my explanation. "Well, Mark, sometimes letting go of the past and trying to work together is the best thing to do."

I wasn't sure if Marcia was talking about my encounter with Jerry or talking about her and I. Either way, I liked her suggestion of working together. I asked her, "So what do you think you and I can do now to make sure Happy stays with me?"

It's funny how I always think I know how life is going to go, or how a problem will get successfully resolved. Yet, I've noticed that life rarely goes the way I think it will go or rarely goes the way I think it should. It seems that the universe has its own plan. Sure, I can try to steer things one way or another, but sometimes it seems like the car I'm steering is on its own track. The steering wheel is just pretend, while life's events are being guided by some other force.

At the time, it felt like everything was up to me and what I decided to do. That was a scary feeling. My track record of sailing peacefully through turbulent waters was awfully poor. I hadn't yet embraced Happy's simple faith that "with love, all things work out for the good." Looking back now, I can clearly see there were other forces at play.

Marcia interrupted my reverie. "Well, the first thing to do is to interrogate your attorney so you know how the law reads. Then, you need to come up with a strategy. Get his opinion on the case. Tell him all about Happy's hurt leg." Marcia was on a roll. "Did you ever find out how Happy ended up at the shelter in the first place?"

I gave Marcia a quick summary of what I knew about Happy's history. I told her the attendant at the animal shelter had her whole backstory. But then I realized I still didn't know some important things about Jerry. Did he have a criminal record? How long had he had Happy? Was he even her registered owner? There was clearly information to be gathered.

As I shared my thoughts with Marcia, Happy looked away. She seemed sad. I heard her say in my head, "The only important thing is honesty and love." At the time I didn't want to hear it. Yet, on some level I knew Happy was right. After all, I had just honestly shared my fears with Marcia. I had taken the red pill.

Having done that, I felt immensely better than if I had avoided being open. But I was new to this "game" of honesty and vulnerability. I wasn't yet ready to proceed that way with Jerry. I would have to go through some very challenging lessons before *that* could ever happen.

CHAPTER 6

Sick as a Dog

As you may have surmised, I don't like lawyers. Whenever I have talked to a lawyer, it has meant that something bad has happened. When my attorney called me a week before the court date, I expected bad news. He delivered in spades.

"You have a minute?" asked Steve as I answered the phone. As an accountant, I calculated that a single minute of Steve's time would cost me about six bucks. But when he'd call me and begin with this "minute" question, it never was for a minute. It was often for an hour, and that was the easy part. The bad news was he usually had something to tell me that would cost me even more. He did not disappoint.

"Sure Steve, what is it?" I responded. I took a seat knowing that he never called me with good news.

"Well, I've been researching precedent in dog custody cases like yours, and I've found out a couple of things. First, there is little precedent, which means a lot of this will be up to the presiding judge. From a legal standpoint, there is just too little information to hazard a guess as to how it will go."

I could feel the knot in my stomach starting to form as he spoke. "Okay" I said, thinking that his news wasn't as bad as I had expected. "Anything else?"

"As a matter of fact there is," Steve began. But before I tell you this, I'm wondering if you did anything recently to piss off this Jerry Lester fellow?"

The knot in my stomach tightened. My mind raced back to the words Jerry and I had exchanged on the phone. I braced myself for trouble. "Well, Jerry called me on the phone last week, and that interaction didn't go particularly well."

"Ahh, maybe that's it," Steve responded.

"Why? What happened?" I heard myself ask in a voice that sounded more anxious than I wanted to let on.

"Well, Jerry's attorney was playing all nice until about a week ago. Then things changed. He's become more threatening and aggressive. Then yesterday I got a signed affidavit from a nurse at Cottage Hospital. This nurse, Ms. Simmons, said you ended up in the hospital after trying to kill yourself. She said you even had to sign a no suicide contract to get released. Is all this true?"

Now the knot in my stomach was doing somersaults. I took a long, deep sigh. I thought of any way I might be able to fudge the truth, but I knew that wasn't going to be the high road. "Yes," I confessed, "that's basically true. But how the hell did they find this out? Wouldn't releasing such records be illegal?"

"Yes it would," Steve assured me. "That's what has me concerned. This guy went through great lengths to get this information. Maybe he knows this nurse personally. I don't know. Anyway, it shows me he's very serious about wanting his dog back. You shouldn't have provoked him."

I felt like I had been punched. Not only could I lose Happy, but I suddenly realized that my own stupidity and lack of compassion could be the culprit. I felt like crying. After taking a few breaths to regain my composure, I finally muttered, "Is there anything we can do?"

"Not at this point," Steve responded. "It looks like you and Mr. Lester have to battle it out in front of a judge. I don't know what a judge will decide between a former dog abuser and a suicide risk. Maybe both of you will lose the dog; the dog may even be put up for adoption for all I know. Do you want me to get more dirt on Jerry? That might help."

I realized that my fearful, nasty treatment of Jerry had already helped to create this mess. Playing tit for tat back at him seemed like a losing proposition. "Nah," I told Steve. "Let's not dig this hole any deeper than it already is."

"Are you sure? It may help your case," Steve suggested.

"Don't do it," I heard myself say with unexpected force. Then to soften my words, I added, "Let's take the high road for once. Taking the low road doesn't seem to work out so well."

"Okay," Steve said. "You're the boss."

I hung up the phone. Chalk up one more example of how talking to a lawyer is even less pleasant than having a root canal. I didn't know what to do, so I figured that telling Happy about the latest news was probably a good idea. She was on my bed, resting on her back with her paws facing the sky. She always looked so blissful when she fell asleep in this position. Evidently she was dreaming because her paws were busy moving as if she were running. I watched her for a few moments, smiling at her paddling paws and occasional muffled barks.

I gently caressed my hand against Happy's belly. I didn't want to startle her. Waking her from a dream to tell her about my real life nightmare was not going to be pleasant for her either. As she reoriented herself to the material world, she gave me a look that suggested, "Why are you bothering me? I was just about to catch the squirrel."

"Sorry to wake you my little poocher muffin," I whispered, trying to soften the transition to reality by calling her by a favorite nickname. "But I just got a call from my lawyer, and he had some bad news to share. I think it's a good idea to tell you about it."

When Happy was fully woken up, I told her what Steve and I had talked about. Happy looked like she was in pain as I went over the details. I had thought that she would use the opportunity to teach me a lesson, or perhaps help to calm my fears. Instead, she seemed to be wincing. When she failed to respond to my update, I asked her what was wrong.

"My back leg is hurting—a lot."

I thought it odd that Happy's only response would be about her leg. Somewhat defensively I said, "The vet told us it would take a while to heal."

Happy looked at me with deep sadness in her eyes. "Well, it's not getting better. It's getting worse. Something is wrong with it."

Happy was not one to complain. One time she got a thorn in her paw and she didn't even say anything about it for a full hour. If it wasn't for me seeing how she was favoring that paw, I wouldn't have even known it was there. My feelings about the call with Steve vanished as my mind was now overtaken by concern for Happy's health. "I'm going to call the vet right away," I told my little girl reassuringly.

We were lucky to be able to get an appointment for just one hour later. I was alarmed to see that Happy didn't want to walk on her back leg as we made our way to the car. Without any moaning, she just sort of hopped on three legs from the house to my car. She could no longer jump up into the back seat, so I picked her up gently and placed her on the seat. Now I was worried. There's nothing like a health crisis to help you quickly let go of all your other problems.

I hate not knowing how things will turn out. In an age where all human knowledge is just a Google search away, all the things you're really dying to know seem to take forever. Earlier that morning, I was burdened with feeling afraid how the court session was going to go. Now as I sat alone with Happy in the vet's office, I was worried about her health. Was she just having a bad day, or was something worse going on? In times like these, my mind always seemed to be my enemy. Unfortunately, I lived within my mind and I didn't have a way to shut it up.

Sitting in an examination room waiting for the vet to see us, I began to hear Happy's voice in my head. It was a relief. Her voice, even when she wasn't feeling well, was much more optimistic than my own. "'You know," she began, "you really need to train that mind of yours. Has it ever been to obedience school?"

I chuckled at her comment. It struck me as funny that we train our dogs to comply to us, and ask for obedience from our kids, meanwhile our own minds rage out of control. "No," I replied, "it's never been to obedience school. It seems to do whatever the hell it wants, and I seem to have little or no say about it."

Happy, trying to lighten the mood replied, "Don't I know it! From what I hear of what goes on in your head, it sounds like a hundred barking dogs."

"More like two hundred," I responded. "And most of them are pretty hungry and mean."

Happy perked up as she realized she was encountering another teaching moment for me. She began, "Well a hungry dog is a mean dog, so maybe you can feed those barkers in your head and things would quiet down a bit."

I looked at Happy. She was obviously in pain, but despite that, she was still looking out for me. I asked her, "Well how do you do it girl? How do you stay so optimistic even though you've been through a lot of hard times too?"

Happy seemed to be thinking about my question for a while. She changed her position so as to put less pressure on her back hip. Finally she answered, "I guess I just do the opposite of what you do in your head. Instead of thinking about how everything could turn out badly, I think of all the good things that can come from what's happening."

I was obviously not someone who looked on the bright side of things. My mind seemed to have a certain question it played over and over like an endless loop. The question my mind habitually seemed to be repeating was, "What could potentially be bad about what's happening?" I could get very creative answering that question. Ever since the call with my attorney, I imagined all the ways the judge could decide to take Happy away from me. Then, when Happy wasn't feeling well, my mind immediately jumped to the possibility of surgery, amputation, or even cancer. Listening to my thoughts was frequently like listening to a mechanical misery-making machine.

In order to distract my mind from its onslaught of fearful thoughts, I decided to ask Happy for her help. Even if her advice wouldn't work for me, at least it would keep me from worrying about her painful leg. "So, my little perceptive pooch, do you have any advice you can offer me to get this barking mind of mine to be obedient?"

"You could always tell it to stop barking."

Happy sometimes said things that sounded like they made sense, but were clearly out of my league. I waved my hand dismissively to Happy. "It sounds like what you're talking about is meditation. I've tried that and it didn't go so well for me. Those barking dogs in my head seemed to get even louder and hungrier."

Happy often had to deal with my objections to her ideas. I once asked Happy a riddle, "What's the difference between you and a Rottweiler?" Happy liked riddles, and quickly said she didn't know. I said, "A Rottweiler will eventually give up." Happy loved the riddle. She took it as the ultimate complement.

Fortunately for me, Happy was willing to try various angles to get around my inevitable defenses. She suggested, "Well maybe you need to give your mind something to chew on. As I've said, a dog with a bone is a very happy dog. A mind with something to chew on can also be pretty happy."

As often happened in my conversations with my four-legged guru, I didn't know what perspective she might hit me with next. I'd think she was going one way, but when that approach didn't work, she'd quickly change to a different tactic. I admired her flexibility. I knew I was the type of guy who keeps barking up the wrong tree just because of stubbornness. For better or worse, Happy wasn't the type of girl to force her methods on me. I always had to humble myself and ask her what she had in mind before she'd tell me.

"Okay Happy, you've teased me enough," I confessed. "What do you have in mind when you say my mind needs something to chew on?"

Happy smiled. She knew I had once again been hooked by her seductive charm. "Well, your mind likes to chew on what could possibly go bad in the future. Instead, why don't you chew on the opposite? Whenever something comes up in life that might cause you to worry, ask '*what could be good about this?*' That's a much tastier bone to chew on, and healthier too. It's as simple as that."

"Yes, it's as simple as that," I repeated while secretly dismissing her words. Yet, the more I thought about her suggestion, I realized that asking a simple question was clearly within the reach of my abilities. To see if this idea could work, I thought I'd give Happy's question a whirl. If nothing else, I could finally show Happy how her method won't work for me. At least I'd have the satisfaction of being right.

Having just received a very distressing phone call from my attorney, I figured I'd try her question with that situation. "Okay," I thought to myself, "what could potentially be *good* about the upcoming court battle?"

Happy heard my thoughts, and had a ready response. "Don't try to pick the biggest bone you can think of as the first thing to swallow. Instead, try it with something small, or something from the past."

"Something from the past?" I said in surprise. "What does that mean?"

I noticed that Happy no longer seemed to be in physical pain. She once told me that the best way to feel better was to focus on helping someone you love. I guess my little girl was practicing what she preached.

She continued, "Just think of some difficult time in the past. How about when you ended up in the hospital after taking too many sleeping pills. At the time, what thoughts were you having?"

I think I saw where she was going with this, but I wasn't sure. "Well, I thought that being in the hospital meant I was a total loser. I thought it meant that my depression would get even worse. I figured it might mean I'd soon not be able to do my job— or even lose my life."

"Bingo!" Happy exclaimed. "You thought of all the bad things that could happen. But what would you have thought of if you had wondered what could be good about being in the hospital?"

"I don't know what I would have come up with," I replied.

"Well look at what *did* happen," Happy explained excitedly. "For one, you found me! You even saved my life. Other good things have happened too, like you are no longer growling at Marcia. You have also learned about forgiveness, play, and love. Looking back you can now see that ending up in that hospital may have been the *best* day of your life."

Happy's words had the effect of pulling the carpet out from my reality. I had been locked into seeing my time in the hospital as the nadir of my life, and she had just made a convincing case that it was the pinnacle. The result was my mind went spinning, and then quickly blew a fuse. My thoughts just kind of stopped. Without so many thoughts bouncing around in my head, I felt very innocent—like a baby seeing the world for the first time. I suddenly realized I didn't really know what was truly a good or bad event within the context of my life. In the absence of knowing that, my mind would just make up stories—usually negative stories-- all based on my fears.

Happy saw that I was impacted, and didn't want to interrupt my rare experience of not knowing. Happy continued to watch me carefully. When she saw I was finally able to take in new information, she suggested I try—with a current example-- her question, "What could be good about this?"

My mind was still feeling blank. I was enjoying the new found quiet. I didn't want to go back to thinking, so I asked Happy to do the thinking for me. "What situation do you think I should try that with?"

Her answer was immediate. "Something not too big. It's good to practice with something small at first. It's like building a muscle. The more you train your mind to ask about the potential good, the more it will remember to do that when times get hard."

By this point, we had been waiting for the vet for almost twenty minutes. Periodically I would have flashes of anger and impatience arise amidst the profound conversation Happy and I were having. I'd think, "Why is the vet taking so long? They must overbook so they can make more money. They're really inconsiderate to keep us waiting so long. Maybe they don't know what they're doing at this clinic." I realized my thoughts were basically an answer to my age old question, "What could potentially be bad about what's happening?" So, based on what Happy had suggested, I asked myself, "What could potentially be good about this?"

Unfortunately, nothing occurred to me at first. I guess my mind had focused on what could be wrong for so long that it just didn't know how to focus on potential good stuff.

Happy stepped in to spur me on. She asked, "Just make up a couple of things. They don't need to be true or even practical. After all, you never know what Grace can do."

I laughed. The first thing I came up with was so obvious that I had missed it. The fact that the vet was taking a long time had allowed Happy and I to have our exploratory conversation. Had the vet barged in five minutes into our talk, I would have missed out on some important lessons.

"Great," said Happy. "And what's another potential good thing that could happen because the vet isn't here?"

"I don't know Happy," I pleaded, hoping she'd help me with a second guess. Yet, she saw through my ploy and didn't take the bait. As I sat in silence, it occurred to me that if the news about Happy's health is bad, at least now I'd be better prepared to handle it.

Happy, hearing my realization, licked my hand. That was her way of saying, "Good boy."

Just then, the vet knocked on the door of the examination room and walked in. We had seen him before, and Happy and I both liked him. His name was Dr. Phillips. He was a man in his mid fifties with a balding head and glasses. He immediately apologized for taking so long. Dr. Phillips explained that a dog had been hit by a car and he needed to attend to him immediately. He thanked us for waiting so patiently while he was able to save this dog's life.

Happy winked at me. She could have told me, "You see? That was another good reason why the vet was late—and you didn't even think of *that* possibility." Yet, she didn't have to say the words. I knew what her wink meant.

Happy liked everybody. She had previously told me she liked Dr. Phillips. Yet, she didn't like being examined. Fortunately, Dr. Phillips knew how to talk to a dog—not in words, but in the language Happy spoke best—love and biscuits. As he examined her leg, he gave Happy plenty of praise and biscuits to compensate for the physical discomfort.

I searched Dr. Phillips demeanor for any signs of concern. He did his best to maintain a poker face. It was clear that Happy was in pain, and that made me very uncomfortable. I thought it strange that when Marcia was clearly in emotional pain, I felt little empathy. However, when Happy was in pain, I became super sensitive. Maybe learning empathy with Happy would someday translate into feeling compassion for my fellow species.

While Dr. Phillips gave Happy a thorough examination, my mind began jumping to possible worse case scenarios. I watched as my mind proceeded to get revved up and out of control like a rabid dog. When Dr. Phillips finally signaled he was ready with his diagnosis, I felt a sense of relief.

"Well," he began, "Judging from the pain she's feeling and a growing bump in her hip here, I think we need to do a biopsy to get a better sense of what's going on."

I didn't know what that meant, but it didn't sound good. The familiar knot in my stomach was back in full force. I immediately questioned the doctor. "What exactly does that mean?"

"Well, I don't want you to jump to any conclusions," Dr. Phillips said.

Dr. Phillip's response made me wonder if he had covertly been listening in on Happy and my conversation. Then I remembered that, unless he was secretly Dr. Doolittle, that was unlikely.

Dr. Phillips continued, "We need more information as to why she has a bump on her left hip. I think the combination of her hurt leg and this bump on her hip is what's causing her discomfort. A biopsy will tell us if what she has is cancerous or not."

My heart sank as I heard the word "cancer." My mind began its mechanical tailspin into a sea of worse case scenarios. If it weren't for Happy interrupting my downward spiral with three loud barks, I might have missed the next thing Dr. Phillips said.

"Now don't jump to any conclusions," he said reassuringly. "It may be nothing. But I'd like to do a biopsy today and it'll only take a few minutes. Once we get the results in three or four days, we'll have a better idea of how to proceed."

My mind was still in a blur. I think I asked the doctor a bunch of questions, but all I remember now is that he took Happy into a back room. Maybe ten minutes later she came back to where I was seated. Happy was relieved to be back with me. She hated needles, and it sounded like a biopsy involved a very big needle. I pet Happy on the head and anxiously asked the doctor if he had discovered anything new.

"No, no, I was just getting a few of her cells to have them looked at. We'll send them to a lab and we should know more in three or four days."

I was going to ask the doctor a lot of "what if" questions. Yet, I knew he would say, "We don't know yet," and I would just be adding fuel to my firestorm of worry. I found it an interesting coincidence that I had just been handed several days of "not knowing" to look forward to. Happy was right. It was indeed fortunate that she and I had been given a chance to prepare for this news. Even though my mind was shouting about possible worse case scenarios, at least I knew not to entertain these thoughts. On the other hand, I couldn't think of anything good that could come from her potentially having cancer. Yet I was able to hold out hope that all she had was just a harmless cyst.

Either way, in three or four days we'd know.

At the front desk to the office, I was handed a bottle of pills to dole out to Happy if she seemed to be in pain. We made another appointment for four days hence to get the results. After paying the bill, I carefully picked up Happy and carried her to the car. She now had a bandage over the part of her hip where Dr. Phillips had done the biopsy. I did my best to make sure I didn't accidently put pressure on that area.

Happy and I drove home in quiet. When we arrived, I carried her out of the back seat, but she insisted on walking to the front door. She avoided using her back leg, and kind of hopped her way to the house. Watching her hop in this manner seemed to be more painful for me than for her.

Once inside, Happy sat down and eyed me carefully. "How are you doing?" she inquired. "Are you asking 'what could potentially be good about this?'

I appreciated Happy's concern. Here she was in pain, and had just been told she may have cancer, and yet her focus was on me. I told Happy I'd try to focus on the positive, but we both knew I wouldn't be taking a deep breath again until Dr. Phillips gave us the results. In an effort to lighten the mood, I said, "Well, this certainly puts the court date in perspective. I guess that's one good thing."

Happy smiled. "Good boy. That's a start. And I'm sure there are other good things than can come from this. We just don't know what they are yet."

I secretly wished I had Happy's optimism. Yet the fact that I wasn't already drowning in self pity and depression seemed to be progress for me. Somehow there was some distance from my usual catastrophic thinking. Thank God for that.

My reverie was interrupted by hearing Happy speak to me. "Why don't you give Marcia a call?," she began. "It's always good to share difficult news with those we care about."

I quickly agreed. Then I realized that something had indeed changed in my relationship with Marcia. Happy was right. I *did* care about Marcia once again. Instead of thinking that talking to her was like getting ready for battle, I looked forward to it. Through a combination of Happy's guidance and my own vulnerability, Marcia and I were clearly no longer in a dogfight. My mind noted that had been another good thing that resulted from all the drama in my life. I thought to myself, "Maybe this question could really work for me." I picked up the phone to call Marcia. There was a lot to share with her.

CHAPTER 7

One Lucky Dog

I DON'T ALWAYS BARK AT NIGHT.

BUT WHEN I DO, IT'S FOR NO REASON.

Four days after Happy got her biopsy at the vet, we were ready to go back to find out the results. As we got into the car, I noticed I was trembling. With Happy's nifty help, I had mostly managed to put out of my mind a lot of the bad possibilities that could happen. Yet, now that we were on the way to the vet's office, the full force of what was at stake was beginning to hit me.

The weather was sunny and picture perfect in almost every way, yet I was experiencing my own inner storm. I knew that a good way to get free from my internal hurricane was to put my focus on my little Golden girl. "How you doing my little princess?" I asked.

"I'm feeling really great." Happy responded inside my head, her eyes twinkling.

I was pleased that she wasn't in pain anymore. The pills the doctor gave her for pain seemed to be making a difference. I surmised that maybe she was even a little high from the medications.

"You are a funny species," Happy remarked. You can make food appear out of a can, and you can make pain disappear with a magic pill, but you have a hard time appreciating even a perfect day."

Happy was good at helping me see that not only was I peculiar in humorous ways, but the whole human race was a bit odd. As a species, we had managed to go to the moon and put little supercomputers in our pockets, but had mostly missed out on the joy that Happy felt so easily.

Happy didn't seem to display any anxiety about our upcoming doctor visit. I wondered if she understood what was at stake. I wanted her to be prepared, so I asked her, "Do you know why we're going back to the doctor?"

"I think so," Happy replied. "He's going to tell us if there's something more wrong with my leg."

"That's right," I began. "And if you have something called cancer—that would be very bad news because you'd need to have surgery, and that can be very dangerous."

Happy looked confused. She tilted her head in her classic "I don't understand" look. Finally, she said, "How do you know cancer would be bad news? Can you know how the future will turn out Master Mark?"

I had to hold back a chuckle. Sometimes Happy and my reality were just too far apart to explain. Although I'd seen the value of asking 'What could be good about this situation?,' that question still wasn't a cure for cancer. Some things in life are just rotten, bad luck experiences.

"No Happy, I can't predict the future," I explained, "but I don't want you to die, and cancer can sometimes be deadly."

"I don't want to die either," Happy assured me. "I now have a Master who can listen to my lessons on love and life. That makes me feel very good. But I trust that whatever happens, it will all work out for the best. That's the power of love."

I didn't want to argue with Happy. Her ideas often seemed naïve to me, but I didn't want to talk her out of her innocent sense of trust. After all, it was one of the things I most loved about her. Even if her world view were wrong or a bit naïve, I clearly needed more of what she had. I couldn't see any benefit to Happy—or to me—of persuading her that being trusting was not always trustworthy.

Once at the vet's office, Happy and I were once again escorted into a private, sterile examination room. I nervously sat down on a wooden bench, while Happy rolled up into a ball on the floor by my feet. To Happy, this visit to the vet was just another event during the day. To me, it was a life changing moment. She seemed to imbue each moment with a similar sense of importance, whereas I looked at life events very differently. For me, most moments were inconveniences I had to tolerate in order to get to a future desired goal. As I sat in the doctor's office, I realized I was once again simply tolerating the present moment. My real focus was on hoping that Happy would get a clean bill of health.

As happened on our previous visit, we had to wait a while before Dr. Phillips entered the room. Yet, this time, I wasn't upset for his tardiness. Instead of conjuring up stories in my head that would make me annoyed or paranoid, I told myself he's busy taking care of other dogs in need. That made me feel better.

"Welcome back," Dr. Phillips began as he came over to give Happy a pat on the head. "Has her pain gone away?"

"Yes," I said, hoping that her lack of pain was a good sign. "Those pills are quite effective."

"They sure are," he responded. Then, Dr. Phillips consulted a clipboard he had in his hand. His face changed as he looked over his notes and the lab results. He took a deep breath before confessing, "Well, it's not the news we would have hoped for."

I immediately felt like I had been sucked into a black hole. My entire body stiffened as my heart sank into my stomach. I realized I had been desperately holding out hope for a clean bill of health. Now that those hopes were dashed, I felt like a trapeze artist without anything to grab onto. "How bad is it"? I finally muttered.

The doctor took another deep breath. "Well, she has what's called a fast growing sarcoma on her hip. The biopsy showed that it was indeed cancerous. Her initial hip injury ended up hiding the sarcoma earlier, so now it's at what is called stage three. Unfortunately, that's the most advanced stage of a cancer before it spreads to other parts of the body. At this point, we just don't know if it has spread.

Dr. Phillips looked at me to make sure I was doing okay. After seeing I was waiting for any signs of hope, he quickly continued. "Of course, there are various treatment options, but the obvious one is to perform surgery pretty soon. Doing a wide surgical excision of the area is the best bet to save her life, and the surgery will help me to see if the cancer has spread to other areas. Yet, even if it hasn't, her leg might need to be amputated."

I felt numb. Thank God for numbness. When I didn't respond to the doctor's news, he softly added, "I'm really sorry to have to give you this news. She seems like quite an exceptional dog."

I looked over to Happy. As her piercing brown eyes stared into mine, she seemed very sad. Looking at her, tears began rolling down my eyes. For better or worse, my numbness had quickly disappeared. I bent over to pet Happy behind the ears so I could hold her close and smell her soft coat. She began licking my tears away as the doctor watched silently.

After a long minute, Dr. Phillips broke the silence. "If at all possible, I'd suggest she have surgery sometime in the next week to ten days. We won't really know if the cancer has spread until we do the surgery. If it hasn't spread but we need to amputate the leg, then we can talk about various prosthesis options. But if the cancer has spread, then we're looking at some very tough choices."

I decided not to ask the doctor about what he meant by "tough choices." I didn't feel like I could take in anymore. Besides, I had a pretty good idea of what he'd say. My father had died of cancer, so I knew that you could always do chemotherapy and radiation, but it often just prolonged everyone's misery for a few more weeks.

I thought about the court date coming up four days hence. Suddenly, it didn't seem to be very important. I wondered how Mr. Lester would react when he'd hear in court that Happy's time in this world might be limited. He'd already lost his dog once. I had the thought that if Happy survived the operation and her leg were amputated, Mr. Lester might not even want a three-legged dog. I was searching for any possibility of good news.

My life as an accountant was always an attempt to bring order to chaos. Make the financial books balance; predict the future as much as possible. I liked accounting because, if you did it well, everything was orderly. Unfortunately, my actual life was the exact opposite. There was always something out of order. Something I wanted to control, but could not no matter how hard I tried. Hearing the doctor's diagnosis had pulled the rug out from under me. I wanted to run. I wanted to scream at God, but when you fight with Reality, it seems that you lose every time.

When the doctor asked me when I wanted to schedule the surgery, I said, "How about a week from now?" Then I remembered to get Happy's permission. I looked at my little girl. She simply said, "Whatever you think is best."

The next thing I remember was reaching home. Thank God my unconscious mind knows how to drive a car—since I don't remember anything about the ride home. As soon as I was settled at home, I gave Marcia a call. When she answered the phone, before I could say anything, I just began weeping. Evidently, I had been holding back a flood of tears ever since I left the vet's office.

Marcia patiently listened to my tears. She had known Happy and I were going to the vet to get the results of the biopsy. There was no need to tell her what happened. After what seemed like a long while, she finally asked, "Would you like me to come on over?"

I blew my nose before answering, "Yes, that would be great."

I hung up the phone and turned to see how Happy was doing. She was once again curled up at my feet. I asked her, "What's up pup?"

Her response broke my heart once again. "I don't like to see you so sad."

Evidently, the fact that she had cancer and needed surgery—and could die—was not her main concern. As always, she was living in the moment, and in this moment, she was very aware of how sad I felt.

"Well," I said, "Marcia is coming over and I'm sure she'll help me to feel better. But Happy, I'm wondering how you feel about your cancer? You'll be having surgery next week, and if it doesn't go well, you might not wake up."

I didn't really know how much Happy understood about death. Although it felt terrible to tell her what might happen, I figured this was no time for secrets. Besides, I thought she might be able to offer up some wisdom that I had not considered.

Happy was slow to respond. I knew she felt sad, but I didn't know if she felt sad for herself—or just for me. At last, she explained, "I understand death. Master Jerry had a cat named Sally that died. It made me sad. It made Master Jerry sad. I don't want to die, but that's not up to me. But I trust that, in the end, love will find a way to heal all wounds."

I once again found myself disagreeing with Happy's naiveté. "But what if you die? What if they have to amputate your leg?" I protested. "Love can't bring a life or a leg back."

Happy stood up from her lying position. She stretched in her downward dog manner, then began, "No, love can't bring a life or a leg back. Yet, it can work in ways that I don't understand. I am not as smart as you Master Mark. Maybe you see something I can not see. Yet, it is also possible that I can sense something that you can not see. I don't know who is right, but in the meantime, I choose to trust and have faith that good things can still happen."

Having lived with Happy for several months, I knew she could understand things that I did not. Yet, I needed to know how to bridge the gap between where I was and where she was. I knew I couldn't just jump into the trust and faith that she had. I needed some tool, some method, or idea that would help me take a leap in the right direction. I asked Happy if she had any words that might help me.

"Yes, Master Mark," she quickly responded. "I have a story and a method that I think might help."

My ears immediately perked up. I was in bad need of some faith and trust. If Happy had some magical formula to help me to tap into such things, I was desperate and ready. She began, "The key to having faith and trust is to see how much we are already being taken care of. If you can feel grateful for all you're already given, then it's easy to feel trusting for how you'll be taken care of in the future."

"Yeah, yeah," I said dismissively. "I've heard that before and that all sounds well and good, but how do I *do* that? How do I feel grateful for all I've been given?"

"That's easy," she proclaimed. There's a magical phrase you can use that will quickly help you feel overwhelming gratitude."

As often happened in our conversations, Happy would dangle a promise in front of my nose. If I was a good boy, she'd give me the key that would help set me free. Yet, she always made sure I was "hungry" for her wisdom before she gave it to me. I was practically drooling in anticipation to hear her "magical phrase" that would lead to overwhelming gratitude.

Happy got close to my ear, as if she was only going to say this magical phrase softly so no one else would be exposed to it. As I awaited her words with great eagerness, I heard Happy say, "Whenever possible, say this magical phrase inside your head: the words to say are.... thank you."

I looked at Happy to see if she was simply joking with me. Yet, she seemed totally serious. Then a wave of disappointment and anger erupted deep within me. I angrily looked at her and said, "That's it?! The phrase 'thank you' is your best idea for helping me feel gratitude and trust? That's it?"

Happy shot back, "No, 'that's it' is the phrase you *have* been using, and that makes you feel like you never have enough. My phrase is 'thank you,' not 'that's it.' The phrase 'that's it' will take you nowhere!"

I was still upset. I looked at her dismissively and then with great annoyance I sarcastically said, "Well, thank you for nothing."

Happy was unfazed. She retorted, "Thanks for nothing," is *not* the magical phrase. The phrase is 'thank you,' and it must be said from your heart. So when you eat good food, say 'thank you.' When you wake up and your body feels healthy, say 'thank you.' When you see your kids or Marcia, say 'thank you' from your heart, and soon you will feel overwhelming gratitude. Once you see how much you're already being taken care of, it's easy to have faith in the future."

Admittedly, I was still disappointed, but I figured I had nothing to lose by trying out her stupid "magical phrase." I recognized that Happy was at least trying to help me out, so I swallowed my pride and sincerely told her, "Okay...thank you." No overwhelming gratitude or angels singing from the sky, but it felt good to not be angry at her. It was a start.

Just then I heard a knock on the door. Happy and I knew it was Marcia. Although Marcia and I had been separated for a year and had gone through all kinds of legal dogfights, it still felt weird that she felt compelled to knock before simply walking in.

Happy, as always, celebrated as if she were being reunited with a long lost love. I greeted Marcia a bit more somberly, but it was still good to see her. Internally, I said "thank you" to myself—from my heart—for the fact that she was willing to come over and that we were no longer fighting with each other.

The three of us made our way to the couch in the living room. Happy managed to find her place between us so she could fully enjoy a petting and love "sandwich." I began silently rubbing

Happy's back. It felt good to touch her. Once again, I thought to myself "thank you" for having such a wise and loving dog.

Suddenly, my mind drifted to feeling grateful for having such a nice couch to sit on. I had long loved my couch, but I had never taken a moment to actually *feel* grateful for it. Then it hit me that I also loved my living room, and my entire house. It was a great blessing to have the money to have my own house. Another "thank you." I was on a roll.

As I looked down at Happy sitting peacefully between Marcia and I, I said a silent "thank you" for having the money to pay for whatever treatment might help her. The next thing I noticed, I had a tear rolling down my face, but it wasn't a tear of sadness. It was a tear of gratitude for all the blessings I had in my life. At that moment, something in me relaxed. What Happy said was true: my recognition of all the blessings in my life helped me to feel that, no matter what happened in the week ahead, things would ultimately turn out all right.

Noticing the tear running down my face, Marcia asked, "So how bad is it?"

For an instant I chuckled. At that precise moment, I was feeling very grateful—even though nothing had changed externally. Rather than explain about Happy's "magical phrase," I simply told Marcia, "I'm just feeling grateful that you're here."

Marcia and I sat silently for a few more moments, both petting and loving on our little furry love sponge. When the time was right, I finally reported to Marcia what the doctor had said. I told her that we wouldn't know if the cancer had spread until she was opened up in surgery. I also told her I had scheduled surgery for a week from today. I included the part about how Happy could lose her leg, or if the cancer had spread, how she would not have long to live.

It seemed that Marcia was a better student of Happy's optimism than I was. With a sense of hope in her voice she said, "So we don't know for sure if the cancer has spread?"

"No," I admitted. "We won't know that until the doctor opens her up."

Marcia heaved a sigh of relief. "Well, I'm grateful for that."

"Me too," I said mechanically.

There was a long silence...

Finally, I revealed to Marcia the "magical mantra" that Happy had described to me. Of course, I didn't tell her how I had received this revealed knowledge. Fortunately, I was able to make up a story on the spot that had to do with reading it somewhere in a book. I told Marcia that it had really helped me to handle the bad news without going off the deep end. I suggested she try it out as well. I figured if we reminded each other to use the "thank you" technique, we had twice the chances of tapping into its power and grace.

Marcia seemed to immediately understand the potential power of the method. She suggested we try a little game. We'd each take turns coming up with something we could feel grateful for. Once something was mentioned, we'd both take a minute to try to really feel grateful for whatever was stated. We decided to each do five rounds of this game to see what it was like.

I began this spontaneous gratitude meditation. I said, "I'm thankful for feeling we're able to support each other and feel like we're on the same team." Marcia nodded her head in agreement. Then we each took a minute to really feel the impact of what I had said. It felt really nourishing.

After a minute Marcia said, "I'm thankful for not being sick today. With all this stress going on, it would be easy to get sick, but fortunately, you and I are currently healthy."

Half jokingly, I said, "Amen to that." Then once again, we took a silent minute to appreciate the good fortune of not being sick. I thought about how rotten I feel when I have a cold or flu, and that it was indeed a relief to feel relatively healthy.

Marcia and I kept at this game for the next ten minutes. We focused on many things to feel grateful for. Some were small things like the weather, our shoes, or the fact that we each had cars that worked. Other things we expressed thanks for were major items that we normally take for granted such as the health of our kids, money in the bank, or the beautiful park a couple of blocks away. By the time the game was over, we both felt "high." Secretly, I gave one last "thank you" to Happy for revealing this amazing method to me.

After the "gratitude game" was over, I felt strong enough to discuss with Marcia some things I had previously avoided thinking about. First, there was the question of what to do about Jerry Lester. Should we tell him about Happy's condition? Should we even let him be part of whatever health decisions we might need to make? My preference was to keep him out of it, but I was open to hearing her—and Happy's opinion.

"I think we need to tell him what's going on," Marcia began. It would be a gesture of good will, and God forbid Happy loses her leg or her life, it would be unfair to not have him prepared for that." Behind Marcia's words, I could hear Happy chime in her agreement.

The thought of calling up Jerry and giving him this news made my stomach churn. I enjoyed being angry and self righteous at Jerry, and I wasn't going to give up this "joy" so easily. "But there's nothing he can do," I insisted. "What purpose will it serve?"

Marcia responded, "It's the right thing to do." Meanwhile Happy transmitted a similar message on the telepathic airways. It was two against one. In fact, my conscience was saying the same thing, so it was really three against one. Despite my sense of dread in talking to Jerry again, I gave in. I told them that I'd make the call. I was definitely not looking forward to it.

CHAPTER 8

Into the Dog House

On the day of the court date, of course I was nervous. However, knowing that Happy was going under the knife in three days took the edge off of how I felt about the court date. As best I could, I used Happy's "magical mantra" throughout the morning. Despite the fear I felt lurking in the background of my mind, my stream of "thank you's" kept me mostly focused on the present. When Marcia dropped by to ride with Happy and me to court, it gave me one more reason to feel grateful.

Going to court over a dog custody issue is quite unusual. When it does happen, it's typically due to a couple getting a divorce. My attorney, Steve, said there was so little precedent in cases like mine that the decision would pretty much be up to the judge's whim.

The judge who was willing to hear our case suggested that lawyers would not be useful or necessary in our situation. The Honorable Judge Melissa Carter made clear that she preferred hearing our case directly from both Jerry and me. We each agreed to the terms. The Judge also suggested that we have Happy available nearby in case she deemed it important to meet the dog herself.

I had explained to Happy the night before what would be happening in court. She asked, "Will I be able to see Master Jerry?" She asked with excitement, but her enthusiasm just made me feel jealous. I told her that she would most likely be able to see Jerry again, but that it would be up to the Judge.

Marcia, Happy and I got to the courthouse and parked. I had already talked to Marcia about taking Happy for a walk, but staying in the area in case the Judge wanted to meet Happy. Normally, dogs aren't allowed in courthouses, but a Judge has dominion over his or her court. If they want something to happen in their court, they can pretty much do what they want.

As I walked into courtroom number three, I eyed a long line of benches with about two dozen people sitting quietly. Judge Melissa Carter was not yet in the room. I spotted Jerry on the left side of the aisle, so I chose a bench as far away from him as possible.

Five minutes later, the bailiff announced, "Please rise for the Honorable Judge Melissa Carter." We all quickly stood up until the judge told us to be seated. I felt nervous knowing that this total stranger would soon be making a decision that would greatly impact my life. I looked at her closely, as if my first impression could indicate to me how things might go. Of course, there was no way to know.

After what seemed like forever, I heard the judge announce, "Would the parties of Mr. Lester and Mr. Mosely approach the bench?" Jerry and I stood up simultaneously from opposite sides of the room and slowly approached the judge. I had no idea what she would say to us, but my stomach churned nonetheless.

"I reviewed this case rather thoroughly, and I must say there is really little to no precedent to go on," Judge Carter began. "That's why I have asked both of you to refrain from bringing in your lawyers, and I am pleased that you both agreed. With so little precedent to go on, lawyers were just going to be a nuisance. Yet, this means that we're going to have to work something out amongst ourselves, rather than rely on what the law clearly states. So I'd like to ask each of you a couple of questions before I figure out how to proceed."

All I could think of saying was "Yes, maam." Meanwhile Jerry remained silent. I flashed a smile at the judge, trying to project like I was the "good guy" so she'd respond favorably to me.

"Let me begin with you Mr. Mosely. First, I'd like to know if there have been any new developments with your dog's—I mean *this* dog's health? I got a note that she was being evaluated for possible cancer in her left back leg?"

"That's right your honor."

"Do you have any new information?"

"I do your honor. Unfortunately, her growth was indeed found to be cancerous. My ex wife and I have scheduled surgery for Happy in three days. The vet told us he won't really know how bad it is till she is opened up."

"Does the vet have a likely prognosis for her?," the judge asked with real concern.

"All he could say is the tumor looks pretty bad, and she could potentially lose her leg, or if the cancer has spread, she would probably not have long to live."

Turning to Jerry, the judge asked, "And how much of this were you aware of Mr. Lester?"

I felt a sudden twinge of guilt. The fact that I had decided not to tell Jerry about the surgery or the latest news on the tumor was not going to look good.

Jerry looked badly shaken by the news. "Your honor," he began, "I knew Greta was being evaluated for a cancerous growth on her leg, but this news about surgery and such is all new to me. I must say it's deeply upsetting." Jerry paused to hold back tears. Finally, he muttered, "I feel I should have been included in deciding what would be best for Greta."

My forehead started sweating. I didn't know how the judge would react. My entire body felt like it had entered a sauna.

The judge turned a stern eye towards me. After what seemed like a long time, she inquired, "So, Mr. Mosely, what was your thinking about not telling Mr. Lester about the latest news about this dog, nor including him in the treatment decisions?"

Before answering I took a deep breath. It was not going to help being defensive or untruthful. Finally I mumbled, "Honestly, your honor, I was scared. I only want the best for Happy, and the whole idea of losing her to Mr. Lester or losing her to cancer is terrifying. Previously I had a call with Mr. Lester, and it didn't go well. I was so devastated by the news of Happy's health that I just couldn't get myself to call him. I guess I should have, but I just didn't have it in me."

Silence. A long, sweltering silence. It's surprisingly hard to truly sit with a negative emotion for ten seconds without resorting to a distraction of some kind. When the judge finally spoke, she said, "Well, I appreciate your honesty Mr. Mosely. I have two dogs at home, and I know how hard it can be when one of them falls ill. On the other hand, your selfishness in how you handled this situation does not speak well to your character."

I wanted to defend myself, but I knew that was a dumb move. Fortunately, I remained silent.

"And my question to you, Mr. Lester is why did you wait three months to find your dog? That seems like a very long time."

As soon as the judge asked Jerry the question, I felt better. I was no longer on the "hot seat." I looked over at Jerry to see what kind of excuse he would come up with.

"Uh, your honor, you have to realize I was going through a crisis of my own making. I was a drunk when I lost Greta. I was put in jail for one of those three months, and when I got out, I felt so ashamed and guilty that I didn't think I was worthy of getting her back. But after a couple of months of going to AA meetings and being sober, I felt like I really could give her the home she deserved. That's when I started looking for her."

"And how often are you going to the AA meetings?" the judge inquired.

"At first it was every day," Jerry responded. Now my sponsor says it's okay to just go three times a week, so that's what I've been doing the last month. I'm 97 days sober."

"Congratulations," Judge Carter said. That's a major accomplishment. Keep up the good work."

I liked the fact that the judge seemed good hearted, but her kind words to Jerry just added to my anxiety.

"Well," the judge continued, "It's clear you both love this dog, and it's clear you both have character issues that could interfere with her care—if she even survives for very long. Mr. Mosely, I see on record that you apparently tried to kill yourself just over 4 months ago. That does not indicate much mental stability. And Mr. Lester, your history of alcoholism and violence also indicates a lack of mental stability. Yet, I believe both of you to be sincere and wanting the best for this dog. Before deciding how to handle this case, I'd like to meet the dog and see how she relates to each of you. It is my understanding Mr. Mosely that the dog is with your ex-wife nearby?"

"That is correct your honor."

"Then I'd like to call a twenty minute recess and have the dog brought in once the court is in session. The court is adjourned for twenty minutes." Judge Carter hit her gavel and quickly got up out of her chair.

As Jerry and I each turned away from the judge, our eyes met. At first our gaze was one of defiance, but it quickly turned into one of compassion. We were both feeling sadness, fear, and a bit of shame. Rather than seeing him as my enemy, I saw him as just like me. We both had our internal struggles. We both had a lot of love for our little Golden girl. We both felt frightened about what would happen to us and to our beloved dog.

I walked out of the courtroom and called Marcia on my cell. She quickly answered and told me that she and Happy were walking about a block away. I gave her the rundown on what had happened.

I wanted Happy to see Jerry before the court was back in session, so we entered the courtroom early. I didn't want Happy to go all crazy with enthusiasm when she first saw Jerry while in front of the judge. That would not help my case.

Telepathically I explained to Happy the situation as best I could. She understood that she was going to see Jerry in the courtroom, but the idea of a judge deciding something for us seemed rather foreign to her way of thinking.

When we entered the courtroom, we kept Happy on a short leash. Yet, before I could recover, she pulled the leash from my hand and ran excitedly over to Jerry. She squealed with delight when she reached him, then quickly placed her front paws on his seated knees so she could more easily lick his face. Jerry responded by letting her lick his face and saying, "How's my little girl? How's my little girl?"

The emotional reunion of Jerry and Happy brought up intense mixed feelings for me. It was always adorable to watch Happy's enthusiastic way of greeting anyone, much less a long lost owner. The normal inhibitions that plague human encounters were not part of Happy's make-up. She let it all hang out. Yet, the fact that she was loving Jerry brought up a lot of jealousy for me. I took a few slow, deep breaths. That allowed me to notice the tears rolling down Jerry's face. It was clear that he really did love her.

After a couple of minutes of Jerry and Happy's love fest, Happy realized that I might be feeling jealous. She looked over at me and Marcia watching her, gave a couple of "good bye licks" to Jerry's hand, then slowly made her way back to where we sat. What an amazing dog. She knew her reunion with Jerry would make me feel insecure, so she immediately began licking me upon her return to my side.

Happy jumped onto the wooden bench between Marcia and I and quickly rolled up into a ball. She looked very content. A couple of minutes later, the judge entered the courtroom from her chambers. Before I could grab her, Happy jumped down from the bench and ran over to the judge's seat. The bailiff tried to stop her, but Happy made moves that would have made her a star running back. Fortunately, the judge was dog friendly. As Happy excitedly licked and yelped in her traditional endearing greeting, the judge patted her and said, "Hello little girl. You're a very friendly girl. I'm glad to meet you."

Before long, the bailiff grabbed Happy by the collar, and gently pulled her back to Marcia and I. I gave the bailiff a sheepish look as I grabbed Happy's collar, and thanked him for his efforts. Before I could berate Happy for her outburst, I heard her voice in my head say, "It's always good to make new friends." I didn't respond to her statement. It's hard to argue with that.

With the courtroom back in order, the judge began. "I asked you to bring in this dog simply so I can see how she interacts with both Mr. Lester and Mr. Mosely. Mr. Lester, can you please approach the bench?"

Jerry walked on up to the witness stand.

"Mr. Lester," the judge began, "I'd like you to call the dog over to you, and Mr. Mosely, I'd like you to release her when he calls."

Jerry clapped his hands together and said in a sing-song manner, "Come here Greta, come here girl." Happy looked up at me, seeing if it was okay to go. I avoided her glance and said nothing. Seeing that I was not protesting in any way, Happy jumped down from the bench and joyfully made her way to Jerry. Having had an emotional reunion with him just minutes before, Happy was less effusive this time. Silently I patted myself on the back for how my "plan" was working.

Jerry pat Happy on the head and told her it was great to see her. Happy was friendly with Jerry, but she was notably missing the frenzied reaction she often met people with. After a few moments, Jerry looked up at the judge and reported, "We had a reunion just a few minutes ago, so she's not as enthusiastic as she was when you were out of the room."

Damn. I was hoping he wouldn't say that. Now the judge would think I had orchestrated Happy's initial reunion with Jerry just so this moment wouldn't look so good. Of course, that's exactly what I had done, but I thought I'd get away with it. I thought to myself, "When will I learn that in life you don't really 'get away' with anything?" Apparently, it was going to take a few more tries.

Judge Carter responded, "Well I can tell she still likes you, and isn't afraid of you, and that's all I really needed to know." Then the judge shot me a glance that silently said, "Nice try Mr. Mosely, but I see through your maneuvers."

The judge announced, "Can I have Mr. Lester and Mr. Mosely please approach the bench?"

Happy had walked back to where Marcia was sitting, and as always, quickly made herself comfortable. I slowly walked up to the judge with a feeling of dread—like I was walking the plank on a pirate ship.

The judge cleared her throat. "Well, this is a most unusual case. I can see why both of you so fervently want this dog. She's incredibly cute and friendly."

In my mind, I practically wanted to scream, "But she only talks to me!" Fortunately, I did not say this out loud. That would have no doubt sealed the case—in favor of Jerry. The judge was already concerned enough about my mental health status.

Judge Carter continued, "Since we don't know what the outcome will be with this dog's surgery, I am hesitant to make any kind of judgment today. It seems that she may not even be alive in a week, but hopefully that will not come to pass. If in the event she needs to have her leg amputated, that may also change the dynamic of the situation. A three-legged dog needs a lot more care then a four-legged dog. With so little precedent and so many possible outcomes, I've decided to not make a definitive ruling today."

Jerry and I glanced at each other, both of us confused. However, the judge quickly resumed her monologue. "Dogs are a blessing to human beings because they are an embodiment of unconditional love. It seems to me that both of you men could use some mental and emotional healing, so I am hesitant to take this dog away from either of you. Therefore, I want you two to work this out amongst yourselves. My hope is that both of you can put the dog's best interest first, and based on her best interest, figure out a way you both can spend an acceptable amount of time with this dog."

This was not what I expected. A bunch of questions quickly arose in my mind, but before I could voice any of them, the judge continued.

"Now on the immediate horizon I'm asking the two of you to decide—together—how to proceed with this dog's treatment. From what I gather, during surgery you may be given some choices once she is opened up. These could be difficult choices. Depending upon what is found, the vet may suggest she be put to sleep, or have part or all of her leg amputated. If such choices are presented to you, I would like both of you to make that decision together. Is that clear?"

Jerry and I said in unison, "Yes maam."

In a stern voice the judge resumed. "Mr. Mosely, if I hear back that you have not let Mr. Lester have an equal say in this dog's treatment, then assuming the dog is okay, I will not hesitate to grant full custody to Mr. Lester. Is that clear?"

I gulped, "Yes your honor."

Judge Carter continued. "Assuming this dog survives the operation and her cancer has not spread throughout her body, you two will have to decide how to share custody. I would accept anything you both agree to. To give you an added incentive for coming to an agreement, I am stipulating that the dog will be put up for adoption in the event you two can not work this out amongst yourselves."

With that last statement, my heart sank. The thought had never occurred to me that I might have to share Happy with my sworn enemy. What would that look like? What would the logistics be? A hundred questions fluttered through my brain.

The judge spoke to my unspoken questions. "Now I'm sure you have reasons why what I'm asking won't work, or you have questions about how to work this out. Yet, I'm not going to answer such questions. The truth is I don't know how all this will work out. What I do know is you both love this dog, and that love is a powerful force for healing. My hope is that your love for this dog will overcome any animosity you have for each other. My hope is that, through your love for this dog, you will work out a solution that is good for the dog and acceptable to each of you. Is that clear?"

I wanted to protest. I wanted to say, "But Mr. Lester abused this dog, and he's a drunk." I wanted to say, "What you're asking us to do is unreasonable and impossible." I assumed Jerry was probably having similar thoughts. Yet, somehow, Jerry and I both nodded our heads and once again spoke in unison, "Yes your honor."

Judge Carter seemed pleased with our minimal response. She concluded her judgment by stating, "I want to see both of you back in court in about a month to inform me of the dog's health and, assuming she lives, your custody agreement. If you come to me without an agreement, I will strip custody from both of you and have her put up for adoption. Case dismissed."

With that, Judge Carter pounded down her gavel. Jerry and I looked at each other for a moment. No words were exchanged, but we both had a look on our faces that said, "Well this will be interesting."

I headed back towards my seat. My legs were wobbly as I eyed Marcia and Happy. They both seemed pleased with the "verdict." I didn't know what to think.

There was no reason to stick around, so once I made it back to my seat, Marcia and I agreed to leave. Marcia grabbed Happy's leash tightly and we slowly walked up the aisle. Before we left the courtroom, Happy turned around and gave two loud barks. The judge and the other people in the courtroom chuckled.

Outside of the courtroom, I was immediately confronted with Jerry Lester. "So Mr. Mosely, it looks like we have some work to do."

In an attempt to start out on the right foot, I said, "Yes we do, so please feel free to call me Mark. And since we will be talking to each other a bunch, I want to introduce you to my ex-wife Marcia."

"Glad to meet you Marcia."

"I'm happy to meet you too," Marcia stated. Congratulations on being 97 days sober."

Jerry looked down at the ground, in a humble 'aw-shucks' manner. "Thank you," Jerry mumbled. Then, lifting his head said, "I've been getting a lot of help so I'm hopeful for the first time in a while." Jerry bent down to pet Happy behind the ears. "In a way, I owe a lot of my sobriety to this little girl. Losing her made me hit rock bottom and finally get some help."

I appreciated Jerry's honesty. I, too, had hit rock bottom before meeting Happy. I knew what that was like. Despite my best attempts at painting Jerry as a bad guy, I was starting to feel empathy for him. Damn. I enjoyed feeling self-righteous, and now I was even being stripped of that emotional crutch.

I was starting to get antsy, and I was ready to leave. I asked Jerry, "So when do you want to talk?"

"Are you free for lunch tomorrow?" he replied.

"Since I work out of my house, my time is pretty flexible." I turned to Marcia. "How about you? You free tomorrow for lunch? I'd like you to be there."

Marcia nodded that she was free. Then she turned to Happy. "Happy, how about you? Are you free tomorrow at lunch?"

We all chuckled. Inside my head, I heard Happy ask me, "Why was that funny? I don't think I get human humor." Of course, that made me laugh even more.

We quickly came up with a plan as to the where and when we'd have lunch the next day, and exchanged logistical information. I was glad the court session was over. While the judges' "solution" just led to new worries, I was incredibly relieved Happy was not taken away from me. I said a silent "thank you" to God and the judge. I tried to put my faith in Happy's statement, "If you put your focus on love and gratitude, good things happen." Sometimes, that's all you can do.

CHAPTER 9

Teaching an Old Dog New Tricks

I had chosen Kody's restaurant for our get together with Jerry following our day in court. Kody's had a nice outdoor patio so that Happy could join us. I figured it would be important to have her with us so I could silently receive her wisdom whenever I needed it.

We picked Jerry up at 12:30. He lived in a one bedroom condo by himself. Just the fact that we were going to have lunch together struck me as miraculous. When Jerry entered the back seat of the car, Happy was there to greet him enthusiastically. He greeted her as "Greta," which always managed to annoy me. Of course, I always referred to her as "Happy," so it was hard to get self righteous about it.

In the awkward silence that filled the car once Jerry was seated, I decided it would be smart to make some polite small talk before diving into a potentially challenging negotiation. "So Jerry," I began, "Have you ever been married or had kids?"

"Not yet," he said, "But I'm always hopeful. It's hard to have a long-term relationship when you're an alcoholic. Now that I'm sober, I'm hoping it opens up new possibilities. But at 48 years old, I admit I'm pretty set in my ways, so we'll see."

To avoid a lull in the conversation Marcia chimed in. "Have you owned dogs before?"

"Oh yes, I've had several over my lifetime, but Greta—as you know—is quite special."

I wondered if Jerry was calling Happy "Greta" to annoy me, or if it were just out of habit. I tried to give him the benefit of the doubt.

"How'd you and uh, Greta, come to meet?" I wondered out loud.

A friend of mine had a liter of pups and asked me if I wanted one. My drinking was getting worse and I reckoned that getting a dog would make me less lonely and perhaps help me control my drinking. Of course, it didn't turn out that way."

Reassuringly, I shot back, "Well as you said, maybe—indirectly—she *has* helped you to stop drinking."

Jerry briefly chuckled. "Yeah, I guess you're right. I hadn't thought of it that way."

It felt good to say something that helped Jerry see things in a new manner. I ventured, "You know what they say: The Lord and dogs work in mysterious ways."

All of us laughed at that statement, and Happy chimed in with her requisite barks of approval.

I was surprised to find I was enjoying connecting with Jerry as a human being rather than as an enemy. I've noticed that people tend to see *themselves* as complex beings that do things based on good reasons, while seeing others in more black and white ways. As I learned more about Jerry, the distance I'd created with him began to shrink. We were much more alike than different, despite my mind's desire to make him into a villain.

When we got to the restaurant, we secured a table in the spacious outdoor patio. There was a Border Collie sitting by the adjoining table, and Happy and the other dog were soon going through their "sniff and meet" ritual. Marcia, Jerry and I watched as these two dogs sized each other up. I've never understood exactly how dogs decide if another dog is an enemy or a friend. I guess it has a lot to do with smell. Of course, I don't really understand how people size each other up either. Many things in life are just a mystery.

I was glad Jerry and I had engaged in some pleasant small talk while in the car. Little gestures of kindness and curiosity like that seem to help lay a foundation for working things out together.

Jerry and I immediately knew what we wanted for lunch, while Marcia painfully poured over each item of the menu. Her slow way of deciding things used to bother me when we were married. I was pleased to notice that it no longer bothered me.

Once we had placed our order, the three of us knew it was time for our challenging negotiation to begin. We all seemed hesitant to start the process. After a minute of awkward silence, I took the plunge to begin. "So Jerry, I'm wondering what your reaction was to what the judge said, and what your thoughts are about the surgery coming up?" I knew I was throwing out a challenging question, but I figured it was best to get directly to the point.

Jerry took a slow deep breath. "Well, I must admit that hearing about Greta's poor prognosis threw me for a loop. I've been feeling really sad and anxious since then. When the judge told us we'd have to work this out with each other, I was still reeling from the news about her cancer. So, I guess I've barely had time to react to what the judge suggested to us."

I appreciated Jerry's vulnerability and transparency. I had painted Jerry as such a villain that now that I was seeing him in a new light, I was starting to feel quite close to him. I confessed, "I'm relieved it doesn't sound like you're holding a grudge. I felt guilty I hadn't told you more about Happy's—uh Greta's—illness. I can understand how upsetting that must have been. I guess what I'm trying to say is that I apologize for how I've handled this whole situation. It has obviously been hard on both of us."

It has never been easy for me to apologize to anyone. Marcia and my kids can attest to that. Yet, somehow saying those words to Jerry felt liberating. It was as if I had been freed of a burden I didn't know I was carrying. Happy, who had been listening to my words from underneath the table, stuck her head in between my legs and licked my hand.

Jerry looked me in the eye and responded, "I really appreciate that. It takes a big man to apologize like that. But, of course, it wasn't all your fault. I certainly contributed to our tension. I regret how I treated…Happy when I was drunk…but I also regret how I've treated you."

Jerry's ability to take co-responsibility felt good, but what felt even better was his calling our beloved little girl "Happy." It felt like a recognition of the special bond she and I shared.

Because I had rarely apologized or taken responsibility for my actions in my life, I did not know or anticipate how good it would feel. I was surprised to find my brain flooded with a release of endorphins. Suddenly, I felt euphoric. The tension between Jerry and I was completely gone, and in its place was a feeling of connection, warmth, and dare I say it—even love. Jerry seemed to feel it too. It was a bit scary and a bit invigorating, like when you first fall in love. Jerry and I both sat silently for a few moments, reveling in the intimacy, and not knowing what we should say or do next.

Happy/Greta finally stepped in. She nuzzled her way between Jerry and I so she could be petted by both of us simultaneously. Her plan worked perfectly. Jerry and I obediently began loving her from opposite sides of her body. Whenever possible, Happy liked to place herself between Marcia and I so she could enjoy what she called a "love sandwich." According to Happy, getting touched and loved from two people at once was the ultimate experience in life. She couldn't understand why humans never tried it.

As Jerry petted Happy's head, and I scratched her butt, the look on her face was one of sublime ecstasy. Rarely do we get to see a being so filled with joy. Fortunately, Happy's look of ecstasy was contagious. We were all getting "high" together, and it felt wonderful.

A month earlier when I was still thinking Jerry was the scum of the Earth, I had asked Happy why dogs were so quick to forgive. She answered in her usual Zen master manner. She said, "People are always doing the best they can at the moment. What is there to forgive?"

I found her answer unsatisfying. I protested, "But how about when Jerry threw a fire extinguisher at you? Was that an example of him doing the best that he could?"

Happy wouldn't budge. She said, "If he could have done better then, he would have."

I was still playing devil's advocate. "But he beat you and damaged your leg. You never got angry at him for that?"

Happy's answer to my comeback, hit me hard. "I was scared, but not angry. Grudges are simply a way to punish someone, but they don't work. They just bite you in your own butt."

I chuckled at that one. I imagined trying to bite my own butt in response to the animosity I had towards Jerry. It was not a pretty picture. Finally, I let go of my self-righteousness long enough to ask Happy my real question. "So how do you think I could someday let go of my grudge towards Jerry and forgive him?"

Upon asking my question, Happy immediately began licking my hand. That was her way of showing me she approved of my inquiry. After my hand was thoroughly soaked, she replied, "If you understand that grudges hurt you, and that love heals you, it's easy to decide to love."

As was often the case with Happy's answers, her prescriptions seemed simple and obvious. So why was it so hard to put them into action? I decided to bring up the topic with Marcia and Jerry.

"I'm really glad I feel like we've let go of a lot of the resentment we've had. It feels really good. Being that a closed and angry heart feels bad and forgiveness feels good, why is forgiveness so hard?"

Jerry was the first to speak. "That's a great question. Maybe we just don't have enough practice in seeing how good forgiveness feels."

Marcia joined in, "That may be part of it, but I think it's more complicated than that. Perhaps holding a grudge had survival value 200,000 years ago, so it got passed down in our genes. But now the world is different. It no longer helps protect us from potential killers. Nowadays, it's much more likely to just raise your blood pressure and give you a heart attack."

I saw where Marcia was going with this. Despite our differences, we used to have great philosophical discussions. She was a true explorer of intellectual ideas. To keep the conversation moving forward, I added, "The world and our society has changed, but for the most part, we haven't. We're still acting like we're in a constant fight for survival, but what leads to surviving and thriving now is different than what it was in the Stone Age."

Jerry seemed excited about the discussion. He inserted, "Nowadays, love and forgiveness are pretty darn good survival strategies. After all, they've worked very well for dogs. Their ability to love us and forgive us has helped them to prosper over pretty much every other mammal."

Marcia smiled before saying, "And now that they've snuck into our homes and hearts, it seems they're doing their best to teach us some new ways."

We all laughed together. For a moment, we all recognized Happy/Greta as our spiritual teacher. It felt good to all love the same being.

Neither Jerry nor I wanted to leave this state of delight, but I realized we still hadn't worked out any of the tough negotiations we needed to attend to. Yet somehow, I unexpectedly realized it would not be a problem to do so. Working out a negotiation with an enemy is close to impossible, but working something out with a friend is a whole different story. I figured I should bring up the task at hand before our feeling of camaraderie faded.

"So," I began, "I guess we have some things to discuss that we need to work out." It was not a brilliant transition, but I hoped it would get the job done.

Jerry took the baton. "Yes we do. As I see it, we have two things we need to work out. First, how to handle what may come up during Happy's surgery, and second—assuming she survives—how to make it so we both can spend time with her. I'm wondering what your ideas about this are?"

I chuckled for a moment before confessing, "I was hoping you'd reveal your hand first."

Fortunately, Jerry took the bait. Putting down his cup of coffee he began, "Okay, here are my thoughts. The vet is going to have more information than we do about her condition and prognosis—especially once she's opened up. I think we should basically go with his opinion."

A wave of sadness washed over me. Although I obviously knew about the seriousness of Happy's condition, I was able to forget about it for long periods of time. Yet now that we were getting into the nitty gritty details of her condition, my fear and sadness were hitting me anew.

Hesitatingly, I began, "I agree it's important to ask the vet for his opinion. But what if he says her cancer has spread and he recommends putting her to sleep?"

I hated to use the euphemism "putting her to sleep," but then again, I couldn't get myself to utter any words about her possible death.

I could tell Jerry felt as uncomfortable as I did. We were both in unchartered territory. Fortunately, we both were touching and holding on to Happy as if she were a life preserver. The feel of her touch and the fragrance of the love she emanated allowed us to continue our way through this treacherous conversation.

"Hopefully it won't come to that," Jerry said reassuringly. "But just in case it does, I think we need to be ready for that possibility."

I nodded silently. Another wave of sadness, and then silence.

Before the silence became unbearable, Marcia broke in, "Excuse me for bringing up hard subjects, but I think it's also important for you to discuss a couple more things. First, how do you both feel about the possibility of raising a three-legged dog? Assuming she survives the operation, that's another possibility. Also, who is going to pay for all of this? Surgery is expensive. So is taking care of a three legged dog if it comes to that."

I knew Marcia was right to bring up these topics, although I secretly was angry at her for doing so.

Jerry chimed in. "Well, I must admit that I'm low on funds. Because I got fired from my job after going to jail, I had a couple of months of no money coming in. I have a new job now, but I'm struggling just to pay my rent. I recognize that since I have less money than you, you should have more say over what happens to Happy—both during and after surgery."

I felt relieved that Jerry would voice that. The night before I had repeatedly rehearsed a whole rant on how, if I'm paying for Happy's care, I should have much more say as to who she spends time with. Having rehearsed my little speech in my head a bunch of times, I had worked myself up into a self-righteous tizzy. I found it amusing that my whole rehearsed rant was quickly burst with a single sentence from Jerry.

"I appreciate you saying that," I responded. Of course, the part of me that wanted to feel like a victim felt disappointed—but I didn't reveal that. Instead, I explained, "I think it would be fair that, assuming Happy survives the operation, we split the costs of her care based on how frequently we each have her. For example, if I had her during the week, and you had her on weekends, I'd pay 5/7th of her care, and you'd pay 2/7th of her care."

I was nervous as to how Jerry would respond to this "offer." It was clearly something I was hoping he'd be okay with. I glanced at his eyes to see if I could get an early read on his reaction. There was no reaction—which just added to my anxiety. After staring off into space for a long time Jerry finally said, "As much as I'd like to fight for every minute with Greta, what you propose seems fair. Besides, I'm gone at work during the day Monday through Friday, while you work out of your home. It would be better for, uh, Happy, to be with you during the week." With that statement, Jerry put out his hand for me to shake.

I broke into a broad smile, and quickly shook his hand vigorously. Happy quickly picked up on our moment of agreement and began licking each of our hands. We both looked down at our little Golden girl who had brought hope back into each of our lives. As Jerry, Marcia, and I looked adoringly at Happy, it reminded me of the time I had gone to a lecture of the Dalai Lama. Somehow, the Dalai Lama had managed to get a room full of strangers to all feel great love and admiration for him. It was clear we were all graced with the presence of a living saint. In a similar way, I felt that Jerry, Marcia and I were being graced by our own living, four-legged saint.

Happy, upon receiving the gist of my thoughts in her head responded, "I'm no saint. I'm just a dog. I'm just a slave to love. Love is the real power."

Happy's words were beautiful, but I had to disagree with her. It's true that love is the real power, but it often takes a being full of love to activate the love in another. Happy was the spark that helped ignite Jerry's and my heart.

There was one more issue Marcia had brought up, but Jerry and I were studiously avoiding it. If the vet called us during the operation and told us the best course of action were to put her to sleep or to amputate her leg, how did we want to respond?

When I brought up this question again to contemplate, Jerry responded, "I'm learning in AA that denial is not an effective strategy. I think both you and Marcia are right. We need to face the possibility that we may lose her, or we may need to amputate her leg."

A flood of various emotions passed through me. It was like going through the famous "5 stages of grief and dying" in about thirty seconds. At first I tried to deny that her death was a possibility. Then, I felt anger at even having to face the question. I quickly realized that such a reaction was ridiculous, so I then thought of trying to make a "bargain" with God. I pleaded that if only her life could be spared, I'd be glad to take care of a three-legged dog. Then I had a vision of Happy as a three -legged dog, and that filled me with an immediate sense of dread and depression.

My mental gymnastics of rushing through the five stages of grief was interrupted by Marcia nudging me back to reality. Softly she asked, "If the vet says it's best to put her down, would both you and Jerry accept that recommendation?"

Having just zipped through the five stages of dying, I reluctantly nodded my acceptance. The thought of Happy having to go through chemo to extend her life a few miserable weeks seemed heartless. I mumbled my thoughts to Marcia and Jerry, and they reluctantly agreed with my sentiments. My stomach, already tied up in a big knot, immediately became double knotted.

Suddenly, I realized I hadn't asked Happy about *her* wishes. I focused my thoughts toward her and asked, "If the vet tells us your cancer has spread and you only have a few difficult weeks to live, is it okay if we…" I couldn't even finish the sentence. It was not clear to me what Happy's concept of death was, and to tell her we could put her to "sleep" would certainly give her the wrong idea. Luckily, her quick response awoke me out of my self-pity.

As Happy looked at me devotedly, she asked, "Would having me die before the cancer fully eats my body help you and Jerry to suffer less?"

It was the type of question that I, admittedly, would never think to ask. As a rather selfish person, I'm usually caught in the mental loop of "what do *I* want?" But Happy was clearly a different animal than I. She consistently showed me what true, unselfish love would look like. It was always heartwarming to be the recipient of such love.

I silently told Happy that it would be easier for us if we didn't have to see her suffer so much. She peacefully said, "Then that would be what's best."

There still was the issue of what to do if the vet told us her leg should be amputated in order to save her life. Many years earlier, I had once seen a three-legged dog struggling to walk, and it was painful to watch. The thought of Happy being burdened with such a fate filled me with horror. Then again, if it were a choice between losing her leg and losing her life, a leg seemed like a tolerable price to pay. As Happy picked up on my mental meanderings, she responded by telling me her thoughts.

"How do you know having three legs—or even dying--would be bad?" Happy asked. "I don't know what dying is, but I've seen Jerry's dead cat and he looked peaceful. And how do you know having three legs would be bad? That's still more legs than you have."

I chuckled involuntarily. Jerry and Marcia both gave me a look that indicated they wondered why I had let out a little laugh. I shook my head to indicate it wasn't worth exploring and they went on talking. Meanwhile, just to be sure, I directed my thoughts to Happy again and asked, "So...you would want to live if you only had three legs?"

I could tell she got my message instantly. Like all good philosophers, she answered my question with a question. She asked, "Would you still love me as much if I only had three legs?"

Her question broke my heart. Happy's innocence always hit me like a loving wave of energy to my soul. I silently answered, "Of course I would."

She promptly replied, "Then that would be fine." She had nothing else to convey on the subject.

I turned my gaze from Happy and looked thoughtfully towards Marcia and Jerry. Decisively I said, "I think if the doctor says her life could be spared if we amputate her leg, Happy would be fine with that."

Jerry and Marcia seemed to accept my answer. Of course, at this point neither of them knew I "conversed" with Happy, but somehow they knew that I understood Happy's innermost feelings.

We collectively heaved a sigh of relief that we all seemed done with this incredibly difficult and unpleasant conversation. While Marcia and Jerry began talking amongst themselves about the café, my mind drifted back to Happy's response to my question, "How *did* I know that her potential death or amputation would be bad?"

In the short time I had known Happy, she had taught me many things. Yet, one of the most impactful things she'd taught me was that my view of the future was often way off base. By asking myself "What could potentially be good about this?" I had become a little less sure of my thoughts about the future. After all, how could I have foreseen that Happy's surgery would help create a healing between Jerry and I? How could I have foreseen that my half assed suicide attempt would lead me to Happy?

I soon found myself feeling exhausted from entertaining all these thoughts. I took a deep breath, allowing the emotions to pass through me. I finally let go into acceptance of the situation. I accepted the fact that things were out of my control. As I let go of holding on to things needing to go the way I wanted, I began to feel a deep peace. It was strange. I felt something I have rarely felt in my life—small and humble, like I suddenly was accepting my size in the universe. Happy's fate was in God's hands, and I would just have to learn to be okay with that. Some things in life you just can't control.

Although I was still apprehensive about Happy's operation, somewhere in me there was something new being born. I guess you could call it faith. Yet, it wasn't blind faith. It was faith based on some experience. It was faith based on something Happy had said to me: "when you put your focus on love, things tend to eventually work out well." The key word was "eventually." I had already noticed that faith didn't mean things always worked out the way you wanted them to. However, I could see that faith in the power of love tended to eventually lead to good things. That was all I had to hold onto, so I held on tightly to this new found faith.

I looked at Marcia and Jerry talking softly. I could tell we all felt small and sober. There was nothing left to do but pray that things would go well. Fortunately, at least we felt like we were all in this together. We had worked out our negotiations. We had forgiven each other. We had figured out what we felt would be best for our Golden girl. We had done our part. Now the rest was up to powers beyond me.

CHAPTER 10

Every Dog Has Its Day

Marcia, Jerry and I all agreed to take Happy to the vet together on the day of her surgery. I picked up Jerry at 9am, feeling relieved that it felt like we were on the same team.

Happy greeted him enthusiastically when he entered the back seat. We drove silently to the vet. It was obvious that we all felt scared and nervous—except Happy. Happy communicated to me that she wondered why everyone was so quiet. Although I had tried to convey to her the seriousness of her surgery, I don't think she really got it. Sometimes ignorance is bliss.

Once we arrived at the veterinary hospital, we announced our arrival with the receptionist, then took our seats in the waiting room. It struck me that Happy was enjoying a reality much different than mine. While she relished the various smells of the waiting room, as well as the joy of having Marcia, Jerry and I all together, we wallowed in fear. To help take my mind off of the potential outcomes I dreaded, I watched Happy as she sniffed her way around the room.

Dr. Phillips came out after a few minutes. We introduced him to Jerry, and he bent down to rub Happy behind her ears. Happy liked Dr. Phillips, and the feeling was mutual. He asked us if there had been any changes in her energy level or how she used her leg, and we assured him there were no changes. The pain pills were still working well. Dr. Phillips assured us that he and his assistant would let us know exactly what he found and what the options were as soon as he knew anything.

I had a special request for Dr. Phillips. I knew there was a chance he would discover cancer throughout Happy's body, and that if such a thing were found, the best course of action would be to put her down. Marcia, Jerry, and I had already reluctantly agreed on that. If that were to occur, I would never forgive myself if I had not said a proper—private—goodbye to Happy. I asked Dr. Phillips if I could be alone in a room with Happy for five minutes before he took her back to the surgery room. He told me that such a request could easily be accommodated. Dr. Phillips asked the three of us if we'd be waiting in the office during the surgery, and we all assured him that we would be. Then, he shook Jerry and Marcia's hand, told me his assistant would call me when a room was ready for me, and promptly left.

I didn't explain to Marcia and Jerry why I wanted to have some private time with Happy before her operation—and they didn't ask. I just knew that I needed to say a few more things to her in case we lost her, and maybe she needed to say some things to me. I imagined that Jerry might have wanted a similar time with Happy, but he never asked for it. Instead, when a woman came out and said a room was ready for me and Happy, I told Jerry and Marcia to take all the time they needed with her before I took her away.

I could see the look on their faces turn to dread. There was no way of knowing if this would be the last time they would see Happy. Neither of them moved for a moment, then Jerry reluctantly called Happy to come to him, and she obediently sat down before him. Jerry didn't want to admit this might be a goodbye, so he simply said, "You be a strong girl in there. We'll be waiting here for you." Then, as a tear rolled down his cheek, he stood up and walked away. He probably knew if he spent any more time with her, he'd break down—and he didn't want that to happen.

I watched Marcia follow Jerry with her eyes as he walked away. She briefly closed her eyes, then slowly opened them and called Happy over to her. Happy sat obediently in front of her, wondering why Marcia looked so sad. Marcia began by petting Happy's head slowly, then rubbed behind her ears in the way that always made Happy look like she was in ecstasy. Then, Marcia bent down and softly whispered to Happy, "Thank you, thank you, thank you." I was pleased that Marcia had somehow fully received the value of the "magical phrase" Happy had taught me.

When Marcia and Happy were done with their little love fest, I called Happy to follow me to the spare room we had been given. Once she and I were inside, I made my way to the bench in the far corner of the sparse room. I sat down on the bench and called Happy over to sit in front of me. I began rubbing her behind both ears. She made a soft moaning sound as I touched her most enjoyable spots. I had a lot to say, but I didn't know where to start.

Finally, I figured if I just started saying anything, the rest would follow. "So girl," I began, "I wanted to talk to you alone because there's a chance we may not see each other again. If this surgery doesn't go well, you may lose your back leg—or even your life. I've been praying that won't happen, but even human beings can't control some things."

Happy just looked deeply into my eyes with a mixture of sadness and understanding. She really knew how to listen, and when there was no response from her, I decided to continue.

"Now in case anything happens to you during your operation, there's a few things I want to make sure you know." I paused for a few moments as many feelings welled up in me at the same time. Once I felt I could continue without breaking down, I softly began, "First, I want you to know that you've been the best friend and best teacher I've ever had. You have brought love and hope back into my life. Every single day that I've woken up with you next to me, I have felt deeply blessed. You are the best girl ever."

Tears starting flowing from my eyes. I let them flow without wiping them away. Happy began licking my hand. It was her way of acknowledging her love for me. Whenever she'd lick me, Happy would get a look of exquisite devotion on her face. Although I didn't particularly like having my hand or face get thoroughly soaked, I never wanted to interrupt her act of devotion—so I'd let her continue. When she finally paused her licks to look me in the eye, I continued my spontaneous speech.

"So girl, I guess what I want to say is how grateful I am for everything you've done for me. You've taught me how to love again. You've showed me that joy and play are more important than just keeping busy. You've taught me that forgiveness and kindness are the true keys to happiness. You have helped open my heart, and there is no greater gift one being can give to another. I am so grateful to you. I love you so much. I love you so very much."

More tears rolled down my face and onto my hand. Of course, Happy quickly licked them up. She had once told me that part of her purpose in life was to lick my tears away. Well, if that was the case, she was very good at fulfilling her purpose.

I had run out of things to say. Happy decided to fill in the silence with some words of her own. "Master Mark, I love you so, so much. You say I healed your heart, and nothing makes me happier than to hear that. You say I taught you how to love again. That's wonderful! But you also taught *me* how to love more fully. You even saved me from dying alone in a cage. You brought me into your home and shared with me your hopes and struggles. You listened to the song of love I tried to sing to you. You fed me, you walked me, you loved me, and you tried to heal my pain. You're the best Master a dog could ever have."

The tears continued freely rolling down my face, and Happy studiously licked up each one as they fell from my eyes.

Once the tears were all licked up, she continued, "And Master Mark, should anything happen to me and I don't get to see you again, there's one more thing I want you to know."

With my voice cracking, I finally was able to whisper, "What's that Happy? What do you want me to know?"

"I want you to know," she began, "that as long as you are loving someone, we will be together."

I was confused by Happy's statement. I gave her a quizzical look, then said, "What does that mean, my sweet girl?"

Happy's response was immediate. "It means that, even if my body is gone, you can still be with me anytime you feel love in your heart. Bodies come and go, but whenever there is love, you and I will still be playing together. So even if I don't see you again, make sure you go and love some more. That's where you will find me."

Happy's words hit me as if they had been spoken directly by God. Perhaps they were. If an accountant like me could channel a wise little mutt, why couldn't a wise little mutt channel the Almighty? As they say, the Lord works in mysterious ways.

At that moment, I heard a soft knock on the door. Dr. Phillips quietly walked in. He looked me over to see how I was doing, then finally said, "The team is all ready for her. Have you had enough time?"

My first impulse was to yell, "Hell no! I need many more years with her." But I knew better than to say that. I nodded my answer to Dr. Phillips, then looked down at Happy. "Okay girl, you be strong. Dr. Phillips is going to take really good care of you."

"I know," I heard her say in my head. "I'm ready."

With that, Dr. Phillips took the end of Happy's leash and walked towards the door. When he reached the door, he turned to me and said, "I'll let you know what's going on as soon as I possibly can." With that, Happy and Dr. Phillips were gone.

I sat for a minute in the room alone. I didn't know what to do, but soon my mind drifted back to the original prayer I had said to God soon after I had taken Happy home with me. On that sacred day, I remember having prayed for the first time in many years. I had asked God that I be receptive to learning from my little girl how to love and be happy again. Well, God had certainly delivered on that prayer, so I figured it was time to pray again.

I never liked the idea of asking God to manipulate the world just for my benefit. Whether asking for a car or praying for a physical healing, I didn't think it was God's job to try to satisfy my latest desire. Besides, how could a mere mortal like me even know what's ultimately best for me? So instead of making a request for Happy's health, I prayed for what I really, really wanted.

The prayer went something like this: "Dear God, whatever happens to Happy today, please give me the strength and wisdom to handle it with grace. May I use whatever happens in a way that leads me to be more compassionate and better able to love others. May Happy be free from her pain and be able to share her love in whatever form she has at the end of today. I thank you God for all you've already given me. I trust that, as I put my faith in you and the power of love, good things will eventually come to pass. Amen."

With that, I slowly walked out of the room. Marcia and Jerry anxiously eyed me across the lobby. With a nod, I indicated I was okay. I walked across the room and sat down next to them and said, "Thanks for that time with Happy. I just needed to say a few things to her." From their silent nods, I knew they understood.

*   *   *

Time can do funny things. A morning spent playing golf or talking with a friend can pass by in an instant. A morning spent waiting for word on whether your loved one will live or die can seem like a year. A long, slow, painful year. As we waited for Dr. Phillips, the three of us mostly tried to do anything we could to keep ourselves distracted from our worst fears. We read magazines, looked at our phones, anything that would keep our minds out of dark places. When Dr. Phillips finally showed up at the other end of the lobby, the three of us jumped off our seats and practically ran over to him.

"What's happening?" I heard myself say as I was still crossing the room.

Dr. Phillips, sensing our anxiety bordering on panic, tried to slow us down. "It's okay," he began. "Take a deep breath and calm down."

I didn't like the sound of that. My anxiety was still at full force. I blurted out, "What have you found out?"

Dr. Phillips began, "Well, I have good news and I have bad news. The bad news is the cancer has spread a bit. It's basically all through her back leg. The good news is it's not in her lymph nodes, and I see no evidence of it anywhere else in her body."

It was now Jerry's turn to ask questions in a panicked fervor. "What does that mean? Is she going to live? Will she lose her leg? Tell us already!"

Dr. Phillips took a deep breath and began, "I'm afraid we're going to need to amputate the leg, but that should spare her life. I don't anticipate any residual cancer if we proceed in that manner."

My first reaction was one of overwhelming relief. I looked to see how Jerry and Marcia reacted, and it seemed they shared my response. The three of us excitedly hugged. While still in our three-way embrace, Marcia and I softly said "thank you" over and over again.

Dr. Phillips interrupted our celebratory embrace. He cleared his throat and announced, "Um, uh, I need to get back into the surgery. I just wanted to let you know as soon as possible what I found. Also, some owners decide to put their dog down instead of proceed with an amputation. So, are you sure an amputation is how you'd like to proceed?

All at once, Jerry, Marcia and I erupted in a simultaneous, "Yes!" I never suspected that having a loved one lose a limb could feel so good.

Dr. Phillips turned back towards the operating room. Before he went through the double doors, he announced, "As soon as the surgery is done, I'll give you a full report."

The three of us glided back to our seats on the other side of the lobby. I was feeling elated, but as I sat there and gradually imagined Happy as a three legged dog, I started to feel sad. I knew she said she'd be okay with having only three legs, but would I be okay with it? That I didn't know.

A week before, I had Googled "dog prosthesis options," to see what the state of the art was. Of course, what Happy could be fit with would depend on how high up the amputation was. The most likely scenario was a harness that went over her back and belly that had a little wheel as a back "leg." It looked pretty uncomfortable, and would prevent her from jumping or going over rough terrain, but at least she'd be able to get around. As I pictured her with the harness on, I felt sad. Yet, Happy had drilled into me that I was not very good at predicting how things might turn out. It was hard to imagine, but perhaps this amputation would eventually lead to something good.

It was another hour before Dr. Phillips showed up again in the lobby. This time we approached him with a bit less panic. "How'd it go?" I blurted out before Marcia or Jerry could get a word in.

Dr. Phillips looked tired, but relieved. "It went well. The amputation was pretty high up on her leg, but I'm confident that this will save her life. She's resting fine. She should be awake in an hour or so. You can see her then."

"Thank you!" Marcia announced.

"Yes. Thanks Doc," Jerry followed.

Dr. Phillips continued, "I'll have a vet tech come out and give you a lot of instructions for how to care for her in the coming week. After a week or so, we'll have you bring her back in and we will fit her with a wheeled prosthesis. Let me know tomorrow how she's doing."

"Yes, absolutely Doctor," I responded. "Thank you again for all that you've done."

Dr. Phillips seemed relieved. He knew how much Happy meant to the three of us. "I'm just glad we were able to save her life," he responded. Then he turned back towards the operating room.

Marcia, Jerry and I took a collective sigh of relief. For the first time that day, I felt like I could finally take a full, deep breath. The three of us stared at each other, not knowing what to do. We decided to sit back down and wait until Happy awoke from her surgery.

Seeing Happy once she awoke brought me to tears once again. It was a great relief to see her physical form. Of course, the lower half of her body was completely bandaged up. Although I knew that her leg was amputated, somehow it still shocked me to see it missing.

The three of us approached her gently, not wanting to disturb her in any way. When she heard us approach, she tried—but failed--to lift her head. As best I could, I sent her the message, "You're okay now. We're here to take care of you."

Happy's response, as best as I could decipher it was, "Thank you. I love you. I'm very sleepy."

Happy stayed overnight at the pet hospital. Jerry had to work the next day, but Marcia and I came by in the afternoon to bring Happy home. There were a lot of instructions to read, pills to pick up, and tips for how to care for Happy during the next week. I was glad to have Marcia there to be another set of ears. I thought that the extensive care Happy needed would become a burden, but as usual, I was wrong. During that first week after surgery, despite spending hours a day caring for Happy, I was elated. Each time I looked at my little girl, I felt grateful for the gift of her presence. Her smell, her form, her every gesture filled me with delight and gratitude.

Within days of her coming home from surgery, Happy and I resumed our fascinating and enlightening conversations. It ends up that, during her operation, she had been gifted with a vision. In her vision, Happy saw that her cancer was part of "God's plan" to help her with her "mission." At first I didn't understand how having cancer could be part of her mission, so I asked Happy to explain it to me in more detail. Our conversation went something like this:

"What do you mean by your 'mission' Happy?"

"Everybody has a mission, although many people forget what their mission is. For dogs, their mission is to love their owners, and to help their owners open their hearts to greater love."

As usual, I was fascinated by Happy's philosophical insights. Her words of wisdom and love never failed to touch my heart. "Well, in that case, you have accomplished your mission my little puff muffin."

Happy's eyes lit up at my complement. "Thank you Master Mark. But I had help completing my mission. It seems that God used my cancer to help bring you and Marcia back together. The cancer even helped to heal the grudge you had with Master Jerry.

Without the cancer, I don't think I could have completed my mission."

I let Happy's words sink in. She had a way of turning what I thought of as "bad things" on their head. Perhaps she was right and the cancer was a "gift" from God. One can never know for sure. What I *do* know is that Happy's vision of how she had been helped to complete her mission gave her much peace and gratitude. My little Golden girl had a lot of faith, and I could see that her faith in God's guiding plan was a better way to live than my own tendency towards doubt. Once again, Happy was acting as my spiritual mentor.

Prior to Happy's surgery, I had worried that she would be very disturbed by her amputation. To my amazement, that never came to pass. Happy's emotional life was based on how much love she could give or receive in any moment. It had nothing to do with how many legs she had. Instead of being bothered by her inability to walk that first week, she seemed to revel in my greater attentiveness and concern. When she got the wheeled prosthesis a week after surgery, it took her a few days to get used to it. Yet, soon, she seemed to be her old self again. It was amazing to watch how quickly she adjusted.

When I asked Dr. Phillips if it was normal for a dog to adjust to an amputation so quickly, he replied, "That's pretty normal. Dogs don't have a concept that they are handicapped, or that this will last forever—so they adjust much more quickly than people do."

Dr. Phillips was right. It seemed that I had a harder time adjusting to Happy's lessened mobility than she did. After all, now I couldn't take Happy to some of my favorite nature trails. As the first weeks passed, I had to keep reminding myself that the important thing was that her life was saved. Happy, on the other hand, seemed as happy as ever. As always, she devoured the sights and smells of life like it was her last day on Earth. To Happy, her back leg had changed into a wheel, but in her experience—nothing was missing.

Happy had once asked me, "Would you love me as much if I only had three legs?" I had answered, "Yes," but it ends up that wasn't really correct. It seemed that I loved her more with just three legs. I found this perplexing at first, but then I remembered something Happy had once said to me. She had told me that love comes from taking care of someone. I think she hit the nail on the head with that remark. Now that she required more care from me, we grew even closer. Her vulnerability helped open up an even bigger place in my heart.

Epidog

It has now been about a year since Happy's surgery. Looking back, it has been an amazing and life transforming year. At first, it took some getting used to having Happy be a three legged guru instead of a four legged one. Initially, I found her "wheeled prosthesis" for her back leg to be disturbing. She'd get a lot of funny looks from folks when I took her for a walk, and I worried that she would miss being able to jump up on the bed. Yet, Happy seemed fine with it all. She liked the special attention having a wheel for a back leg brought her. She told me, "Being a dog with a handicap is even better for opening human hearts than just being a dog." My little girl always managed to see the silver lining in whatever situation she happened to be in.

After a few months, the vet was able to fit Happy with a specially made prosthesis, and the wheel was no longer necessary. I was hoping her new prosthesis would blend in with her coat, but Happy insisted it be painted bright pink—so she'd still get special attention for being handicapped. Anytime we'd pass a child with a disability, Happy would make sure to show off her fake leg. She said it always made handicapped kids feel better about themselves.

This past year brought lots of other changes too. Not only did my joint custody arrangement with Jerry go well, but we've even become good friends. From where we started, I would have never guessed that could have happened. Fortunately, Jerry is now almost 500 days sober, and we've even gone to many AA meetings together. Although I was never a fall down drunk, I decided to give up alcohol. I figure for someone like me, alcohol was more of a crutch than a pleasure. It feels good to now know I have the tools to deal with life's challenges in healthier ways.

Another massive change that has occurred is the fact that Marcia and I are back living together. I must confess, I didn't see that one coming either. Somehow, all the time we spent together before and after Happy's surgery ended up rekindling our love. I have often joked with Marcia that she really wanted to live with Happy, and I was just part of the bargain. There's probably some truth in that, but I don't care. We're doing well together. Whenever there's a problem, Happy gets between us and reminds us that what is truly important is not who is right and who is wrong, but who is the most loving.

But perhaps the biggest change in my life has been the fact that, for the first time in a long while, I'm pretty happy. That may not sound like much, but for a historically "mopey mutt" such as myself, that's a fricken miracle. When I ponder how this miracle occurred, I have to give almost all the credit to my little Golden girl. After all, she was the one that taught me the healing power of love. She also taught me to look on the bright side by asking, "What could be good about this?" She even taught me the simple, but life transforming power of feeling gratitude and saying "thank you" from the heart many times a day. She has truly been my guru.

I guess you could say I've been on quite a journey—from suicidal depression and loneliness, to greater happiness and connection. In a way, we're all just trying to find some joy and happiness in life, but in this day and age, it's pretty easy to get sidetracked. That's why it's so important to be open to the simple wisdom of our pets, as well as our kids. Through their innocence, openness, and love, they remind us that life is a gift to be enjoyed and treasured with others.

I never considered myself to be a writer. Yet, I felt like Happy's life lessons were too precious to keep all to myself. When I finally told Jerry and Marcia that I could hear Happy's voice in my head, I was surprised at their reaction. I feared they would think I'd gone off the deep end again, but instead, they were just very curious. I guess they sensed she and I had always had some kind of special bond, so it actually made sense to them that this "gift from God" had occurred. Of course, I'm sure some people will think I'm crazy, but if Happy's wisdom can sneak into their heart through my story, then it'll all be worth it.

Recently, I asked Happy if she would come up with a few simple suggestions--or even commandments--to help humans along their journey to greater happiness. She was thrilled to do so. After a few moments of silence, she revealed her ten commandments for a truly fulfilling life. I studiously jotted them down for your amusement and benefit:

Happy's Ten Commandments for a Joyous Life:

1. Explore and enjoy whatever is in front of you in this moment.
2. Eat with gusto.
3. Love everyone you meet as long as they don't try to bite you.
4. Make sure you pee in lots of different locations.
5. Play every single day, and chew on things as much as you can.

6. Whenever possible, take a nap.

7. Ask directly for belly rubs and whatever affection you desire.

8. Never hold a grudge; each moment is new.

9. Stop and smell the roses, as well as everything else.

10. Greet those you love with great enthusiasm when they come home.

May Happy's commandments help guide you and your loved ones toward an ever more fulfilling life...

About the Author

Jonathan Robinson is the author of thirteen books, a psychotherapist and life coach. He has appeared numerous times on *Oprah*, as well as on *The Today Show, and CNN*.

His books include *Find Happiness Now, Opening to the Infinite, The Technology of Joy,* and *Communication Miracles for Couples*.

As a professional speaker, Jonathan conducts seminars and keynotes for businesses, church groups, and corporations such as Google, Coca-Cola, and Microsoft. His topics range from overcoming stress and increasing productivity, to achieving life balance and effective communication. Jonathan is known for providing people with practical ideas and methods presented in an entertaining manner.

Jonathan co-hosts a popular podcast called "Awareness Explorers" (on iTunes and at AwarenessExplorers.com). In his free time, Jonathan enjoys coaching people to greater happiness and success, and playing with his two dogs: Sophie and Bailey. His web site is FindingHappiness.com and his email address is iamjonr@aol.com

GO TO: www.FindingHappiness.com TO GET THE ABSOLUTE BEST WAYS TO EASILY BOOST HAPPINESS IN UNDER TWO MINUTES.